The Truth
Shall Make
You Free

Gustavo Gutiérrez

The Truth
Shall Make
You Free

CONFRONTATIONS

Translated from the Spanish by
Matthew J. O'Connell

ORBIS BOOKS

Maryknoll, New York 10545

The Catholic Foreign Mission Society of America (Maryknoll) recruits and trains people for overseas missionary service. Through Orbis Books, Maryknoll aims to foster the international dialogue that is essential to mission. The books published, however, reflect the opinions of their authors and are not meant to represent the official position of the society.

This is a slightly revised edition of *La verdad los hará libres: confrontationes*, © 1986 by Instituto Bartolomé de Las Casas, Ricardo Bentí in 763 - Apartado 3090, Lima 25, Peru, and Centro de Estudios y Publicaciones (CEP), Lampa 808, of. 601 - Apartado 6118, Lima, Peru

English translation © 1990 by Orbis Books, Maryknoll, NY 10545
All rights reserved
Manufactured in the United States of America

Manuscript editor: William E. Jerman

Library of Congress Cataloging-in-Publication Data

Gutiérrez, Gustavo, 1928-
 [Verdad los hará libres. English]
 The truth shall make you free : confrontations / Gustavo Gutiérrez; translated from the Spanish by Matthew J. O'Connell.
  p. cm.
 Translation of: La verdad los hará libres.
 Includes bibliographical references.
 ISBN 0-88344-679-0 — ISBN 0-88344-663-4 (pbk.)
 1. Liberation theology. 2. Theology—Methodology. 3. Church work with the poor. I. Title.
 BT83.57.G88413 1990
 230'.2—dc20   90-30553
                                                  CIP

Contents

Presentation

I heartily welcome this English translation of writings in which my friend, Father Gustavo Gutiérrez, presents a synthesis of his thought as he has honed it through personal prayer, dialogue, and response to much negative criticism. He also has the opportunity to answer his critics in solid fashion and with a peaceful tone so characteristic of his person. He clearly demonstrates that his theological position not only conforms to the teaching of the Roman Catholic Church but is also in line with the spirit of the Church today as it is faced with the difficult task of becoming a church of and for the poor.

Interesting to the critics of Gutiérrez's exposition of liberation theology is his response to charges that his work is influenced by Marxism. He conclusively points out that "class struggle," which he calls "social conflict," is not the driving mechanistic force of history. Though social conflict is an unfortunate fact of life, Christians who struggle for social change must not be motivated by hatred. Further, he points out that an economically based determinist view of class struggle is completely alien to liberation theology. Characteristic of his deep spirituality is his belief that because genuine liberation is liberation from sin, then Jesus Christ is the true Liberator.

I believe that all those who are making a real effort to understand the option for the poor and liberation theology will be greatly helped by this book.

Most Rev. Peter A. Rosazza
New Haven, Connecticut

Foreword

I have been a friend of Gustavo Gutiérrez for about forty years, having first known him as a young premedical student and a member of the young men's section of Peruvian Catholic Action.

In the study clubs that were popular at that time, commentary on the gospel followed the guidelines given by the pope, Pius XII; we studied the great encyclicals of that same pope. We also used the works of Romano Guardini and Karl Adam, and read the forceful editorials in the Argentinean periodical *Criterio*, of which Gustavo J. Franceschi was editor-in-chief.

A sincere and loyal love of the church pervaded the commentaries on Pope Pacelli's encyclical on the Mystical Body of Christ, wherein he studied in depth the Pauline idea that all of us, although our roles differ, are members of the church. Guardini's desire that this might become "the century of the church" was being brought to fulfillment. It impelled us to make our membership in the church truly part of ourselves and it sowed the seeds of an unchanging fidelity to our Lord Jesus Christ and his Mystical Body, a fidelity inseparable from love of the eucharist.

Reflection and conversations with his teachers, César Arróspide and Gerardo Alarco, led Gustavo to a new commitment; he abandoned the study of medicine at the University of San Fernando and of letters at the Catholic University and went instead to Santiago de Chile where he began the study of philosophy in the seminary.

He then went to Louvain to study philosophy; inspired by his earlier interest in medicine he also studied psychology, producing an interesting piece of work on Freudian psychoanalysis. He passed on from this to the study of theology, first at Lyons and then, as an ordained priest, at Rome.

He kept his close ties to the university world and taught in the department of theology at the Catholic University, while also serving as advisor to university students of the National Union of Catholic Students.

"The social requirements of Catholicism" as expounded in a timely and beautiful pastoral letter of the Peruvian episcopate in 1958 and further explained at the First Social Week the following year provided directives for the lay apostolate that were welcomed especially by university students.

Gutiérrez's theological thinking, in close contact with the realities of society in our country, and his desire as a scholar to find ways of helping our Peruvian people in their miserable state, developed in study clubs, lectures, and conversations, a course of action that is now familiar to all the world and has made Gustavo well known as a profound thinker.

Amid all the ups and downs—the successes and applause, the misunderstandings and opposition—Gustavo Gutiérrez has been able, even in times of suffering, to preserve the fidelity to the church that he learned as a youth.

The present book is one more proof of the loyal and deeply rooted witness that he gives in all his intellectual and pastoral work.

José Dammert Bellido
Archbishop of Cajamarca

Chapter One

A Discussion of Gustavo Gutiérrez's Work (Lyons, 1985)

INTRODUCTION

On May 29, 1985, Father Gustavo Gutiérrez received a doctorate in theology from the theological faculty of the Catholic Institute of Lyons, where he had done his theological studies. The "dissertation" he submitted was not a single piece of scholarship but the body of work he had published up to that point: Lineas pastorales de la Iglesia Latinoamericana *(1970);* Teología de la liberación *(1971;* A Theology of Liberation, *1973, new ed., 1988);* Liberation and Change *(with R. Shaull; 1977);* La fuerza histórica de los pobres *(1979;* The Power of the Poor in History, *1983);* El Dios de la vida *(1982);* Beber en su propio pozo *(1983;* We Drink from Our Own Wells, *1984); and numerous articles.*

Gérard Defois, rector of the institute, presided at the defense. The members of the jury were: Henri Bourgeois, dean of the faculty; Maurice Jourjon, patrologist and honorary dean of the faculty; Christian Duquoc, O.P., director of the dissertation, known for his own work on christology; Jean Delorme; Bernard Sesboüé, S.J., of the Centre-Sèvres in Paris, dean of the Theological Faculty there, and member of the International Theological Commission; and Vin-

1

cente Cosmao, director of the Centre Lebret and member of the Pontifical Commission for Justice and Peace.

A "defense of a dissertation," at Lyons, has two parts. The first, which takes place in the morning, consists of a professorial lecture; in this case, Father Gutiérrez chose as his subject "Theology and Spirituality," a theme he had developed at length in his book We Drink from Our Own Wells. The second part takes place in the afternoon and consists of a discussion with the jury. Father Gutiérrez began the dialogue by offering a summary of the theological viewpoints expressed in his various works; this is the text translated here under the title "Presentation of the Dissertation." The members of the jury then asked Father Gutiérrez a number of questions that led to an interesting discussion that lasted over four hours; a summary of it, based on the record kept of the proceedings, is presented here as "The Discussion."

At the end of the discussion—which became, as Father Duquoc hoped it would, an academic dialogue between European theology and the theology of liberation—the jury granted Father Gustavo Gutiérrez the degree of Doctor of Theology. They granted it with the qualification summa cum laude, the highest qualification possible and one that is given only when the jurors are in unanimous agreement.

Since the text that follows is the presentation of a dissertation based on the works listed above, readers will find in it echoes of other articles by the author. It seemed appropriate, nonetheless, to include the presentation because it summarizes the author's thinking and provides a panoramic view of his work and because the discussion that follows the presentation represents an interesting debate in the field of contemporary theology.

PRESENTATION OF THE DISSERTATION

I should like to set forth in plain language the points I regard as central and constant in the publications I am offering as a dissertation for the doctorate in theology.[1]

A LANGUAGE FOR SPEAKING OF GOD

Thinking the Mystery

Every theology is talk about God; in the final analysis, God is its only subject-matter. On the other hand, the God of Jesus

Christ is presented to us as a mystery; a sound theology is therefore conscious of attempting something difficult, not to say impossible, when it seeks to think this mystery and speak about it. This fact accounts for the well-known statement of Thomas Aquinas: "We cannot know what God is, but only what God is not." It is important to be clear on this point at the beginning of any formal treatment of faith. José María Arguedas, a Peruvian writer, made the same point, though outside a strictly theological framework, when he said: "What we know is far less than the great hope we feel." In very truth, God is an object less of knowledge than of hope respectful of the mystery.

At the same time, however, God is a mystery that must be communicated and may not be left hidden, because it means life for every human being. How, then, are we to find a way of speaking about God?

Adopting the viewpoint of the theology of liberation, I will say that we must begin by contemplating God and doing God's will and that only in a second step are we to think about God. By this I mean that worship of God and the doing of God's will are the necessary condition for thinking about God. Only if we start in the realm of practice will we be able to develop a discourse about God that is authentic and respectful.

In our dealings with the poor we encounter the Lord (see Mt. 25:31–46), but this encounter in turn makes our solidarity with the poor more radical and more authentic. Contemplation and commitment within history are fundamental dimensions of Christian practice; thus there is no way of evading them. The mystery reveals itself through prayer and solidarity with the poor. I call Christian life itself the "first act"; only then can this life inspire a process of reflection, which is the "second act."

Contemplation and commitment combine to form what may be called the phase of *silence* before God. Theological discourse, on the other hand, is a *speaking* about God. Silence is a condition for any loving encounter with God in prayer and commitment. Experience of the inadequacy of words to express what we live out in our depths will make our speech both more fruitful and more unpretentious. Theology is talk that is constantly enriched by silence.

The great hermeneutical principle of faith and, therefore, of all theological discourse is Jesus Christ. He is the revealer of the Father; in him all things have been created and redeemed (see Col. 1:15–20). The incarnation of the Son of God is the basis for the hermeneutical circle: from human being to God and from God to human being, from history to faith and from faith to history, from human words to the word of the Lord and from the word of the Lord to human words, from love of our brothers and sisters to love of the Father and from love of the Father to love of our brothers and sisters, from human justice to the holiness of God and from the holiness of God to human justice. Christ, the Word of the Father, is the center of all theology, of all talk about God.

Theology is a critical reflection, in the light of the divine word received in faith, on the presence of Christians in the world. As such, it must help us to see how we are to relate the life of faith to the demands made upon us by the building of a human and just society. It will make explicit the values of faith, hope, and charity contained in this commitment. But it will also be the function of theology to correct possible deviations, as well as to keep Christians mindful of some aspects of Christian life that they risk forgetting if they allow themselves to be carried away by the requirements of direct political action, however much inspired by generosity.

Such is the task of a critical reflection that, by definition, is unwilling to settle for being an a posteriori justification of what Christians do. In the final analysis, theology helps make service of the church's evangelizing mission more evangelical, more concrete, more effective. Theology is in the service of the church's work of evangelization and develops within it as an ecclesial function.

Spirituality and Theological Method

The distinction of two phases (first act and second act) is a key element in theological method—that is, in the procedure ("method" is derived from Greek *hodos* = "way") that must be followed for reflecting in the light of faith. The point is certainly more traditional than many suspect, but what needs to be emphasized here is that it is not a matter simply of theological methodology but rather implies a lifestyle, a way of being and of becoming a disciple of Jesus.

In the book that tells us of the Acts of the first Christian community, the Christian manner of life is given a particular and original name: "the way." The word is used without any further qualification. To "follow the way" means to conduct oneself in a certain manner; the Greek word *hodos* can mean both conduct and way or path. Christians are distinguished by their behavior, their lifestyle. This sets the Christian community apart in both the Jewish and the pagan worlds in which it lives and bears witness. Its behavior consists in a way of thinking and acting, of "walking according to the Spirit" (see Rom. 8:4).

The course to be followed if one is to be a Christian is the basis for the direction in which one must move in order to do theology. It can therefore be said that our methodology is our spirituality (that is, our way of being Christians). Reflection on the mystery of God can be undertaken only by following in the footsteps of Jesus. Only if we begin by walking according to the Spirit can we think and proclaim the love freely bestowed by the Father on every human being. Perhaps it is because of this connection between Christian life and theological method that the basic ecclesial communities of Latin America are playing an increasingly active role in this development of a theology.

All Christian life begins with a conversion. This means a break with personal and social sin and a launching out on a new path. Such a conversion is a condition for, and a demand made by, reception of the gift of God's kingdom (see Mk. 1:14). Conversion means leaving one's own way (see Lk. 10:25–37) and entering upon the way of the other, the neighbor, and especially of the poor in whom we encounter the Lord (see Mt. 25:31–45). Conversion is also a condition for anything more than superficial theological activity.

Entrance into the world of the poor is a long and sometimes painful process, but it is there that we find the One of whom theology is called upon to speak. In addition to being difficult, the process entails risks, for this speech, which is speech about the God of life, means challenging at its root a world stamped by death and injustice.

All theology starts with the act of faith. In this context, how-

ever, "faith" is understood not simply as an intellectual acceptance of the message but also as a vital reception of the gift of
the divine word heard in the ecclesial community, as an encounter with the Lord, and as love for our brothers and sisters. At
issue is our entire existence. Acceptance of the word, a turning
of the word into life and concrete action: this stands at the
beginning of any understanding of the faith.

Here we see the real meaning of St. Anselm's words: "I
believe in order that I may understand," as he himself explains
them in a well-known passage:

> Lord, I am not attempting to plumb your depths, for my
> mind could not possibly exhaust your being; but I do desire
> to understand to some extent your truth in which my heart
> believes and which it loves. I do not seek to understand in
> order to believe, but rather I believe in order that I may
> understand. For I am certain that if I do not believe, I will
> not understand [*Proslogion*, end of chapter 1].

The primacy of God and the grace of faith give the work of
theology its raison d'être. In that light we realize that if Christians seek to understand their faith, they do so, in the final
analysis, in order to be able to "follow Christ"—that is, to feel,
think, and act as he did. An authentic theology is always a spiritual theology as understood by the fathers of the church. All
this means that the life of faith is not only the starting point of
theological reflection but also its point of arrival. There is thus
a circular relationship between faith and understanding.

A Christian is defined as one who follows Christ. But according to the biblical sources the following is a communal experience, for it is really a people that sets out on a journey. The
poor of Latin America are today taking an active part in the
struggle to assert their human dignity and their status as sons
and daughters of God, and in this activity a spiritual experience
is unfolding. In other words, the struggle is the place and time
of an encounter with the Lord; a way is opening up therein for
the following of Jesus Christ.

The fontal character of the *sequela Christi* is already a long-
standing concern in Latin American theological thought

(because the latter is conscious of being preceded by the spiritual experience of Christians committed to the process of liberation). But the concern has become more urgent and richer in the rush of events in recent years. In the context of the struggle for liberation, which seeks to establish love and justice among all, a new way is perhaps opening up for the following of Jesus in Latin America. This spirituality is in a germinal stage and for that very reason eludes precise definition and any attempt to describe and capture it with a few strokes; but it is not therefore any less real and promising.

The Historical Starting Point

Ever since the Enlightenment a large sector of modern theology has taken as its point of departure the challenge launched by the modern (often unbelieving) mind. That mind confronts our world of religion and calls for a radical purification and renewal of it. Bonhoeffer took up the challenge and formulated in a penetrating way the question that is at the origin of a number of theological undertakings in our time: "How are we to proclaim God in a world come of age?"

But in Latin America the challenge does not come first and foremost from nonbelievers but from nonpersons—that is, those whom the prevailing social order does not acknowledge as persons: the poor, the exploited, those systematically and lawfully stripped of their human status, those who hardly know what a human being is. Nonpersons represent a challenge, not primarily to our religious world but to our economic, social, political, and cultural world; their existence is a call to a revolutionary transformation of the very foundations of our dehumanizing society.

In this context, then, the question is not: How are we to talk of God in a world come of age?, but: How are we to proclaim God as a Father in a nonhuman world? What is implied when we tell nonpersons that they are sons and daughters of God? These questions were the ones being asked, in one or other fashion, back in the sixteenth century by Bartolomé de Las Casas and many others once they had come into contact with the native Americans.

In other words, the question being raised today in Latin America is this: How are we to speak of God in face of the suffering of the innocent? This is more or less the theme of the Book of Job. We can in fact claim that a language for speaking about God is arising among us today out of the unjust sufferings, but also the hopes, of the poor of Latin America.

FROM THE UNDERSIDE OF HISTORY

The Irruption of the Poor
It can be said that in recent decades the church's life and thought in its Latin American setting have been marked by what we may call "the irruption of the poor." This phrase means that those who until now were "absent" from history are gradually becoming "present" in it. This new presence of the poor and oppressed is making itself felt in the popular struggles for liberation and in the historical consciousness arising from these struggles. It is also making itself felt within the church, for there the poor are increasingly making their voices heard and claiming openly their right to live and think the faith in their own terms. The rise of the basic ecclesial communities is one expression of this phenomenon (Puebla, nos. 93, 643, 1147); the theology of liberation is another (see the Document of the Peruvian Episcopal Conference on the Theology of Liberation, 1984, no. 20).

The poor who are irrupting into our history are a people both oppressed and Christian. Latin America is in fact the only constituent part of the so-called Third World that has a majority of Christians. This makes the situation especially painful and constitutes a major challenge to the Christian faith and to the church.

"Oppressed" and "Christian" are two aspects of one and the same people. This means that it is impossible to take one aspect into account without connecting it with the other, as some have wanted to do. The Christian character of the Latin American people is affected by the condition of oppression in which they live; conversely, their faith puts its mark both on their experience of injustice and on their quest for ways of freeing themselves from the situation.

In saying this, I am not doing away with the difference between the two dimensions or aspects, but simply trying to underscore the way in which they are experienced in the concrete life of a people. Consequently, the adoption of this viewpoint entails opposition to every kind of "reductionism." It has been a concern of the theology of liberation from the very beginning to reject, on the one hand, a disincarnate spiritualism that emphasizes the religious side of a people without attending to the material conditions in which they live, and, on the other, a political activity that sets aside until later the requirements and possibilities of the Christian faith, on the grounds that economic and social problems are more urgent. (These are nevertheless two persistent temptations; see Puebla, no. 329; for this reason the Instruction of September 1984 warns against "the temptation to reduce the gospel to an earthly gospel" [VI, 5; see also VI, 4]. But it is important that this observation not be taken as approbation "of those who contribute to the misery of the people" [XI, 1].) These two kinds of reductionism ignore both the fulness of the Christian message and the concrete life of the Latin American people. They refuse to see that the great challenge we must face is to learn to encounter the Lord in today's poor. The challenge, in other words, is to live a hope-filled and joyous faith within a love that creates solidarity with the oppressed and their hopes and struggles, with a view to their complete liberation.

The World of the Poor

The Latin American situation is characterized by a poverty that Puebla calls "the most devastating and humiliating kind of scourge" (no. 29) and "anti-evangelical" (no. 1159). In the well-known phrase of Medellín, the situation is one of "institutionalized violence" (*Peace*, no. 16). It therefore becomes necessary to analyze and denounce the structural causes of the injustice and oppression in which the poor of Latin America are living. For as John Paul II reminded us at Puebla, "there are mechanisms which produce an international system in which the rich become ever richer at the expense of the poor becoming ever poorer" (Opening Address at Puebla, III, 4).

We are becoming increasingly aware today of what is at stake in this situation—namely, that poverty means death. Death, in this case, is caused by hunger, sickness, or the oppressive methods used by those who see their privileges endangered by any and every effort to free the oppressed. It is physical death to which cultural death is added, because in a situation of oppression everything is destroyed that gives unity and strength to the dispossessed of this world. Here is where the theological undertaking known as the theology of liberation applies social analysis, with the intention that it help us understand the concrete forms that injustice and death take in Latin America.

It is of all this that we are speaking when we talk of poverty and the destruction of individuals and peoples, of cultures and traditions. We are speaking especially of the poverty of the most deprived: Amerindians, blacks, and women, these last being doubly marginalized and oppressed if they are also Amerindian or black. We are not therefore, as has been claimed at times, confronting only the challenge of a "social situation," as if it were something that had nothing to do with the fundamental demands of the gospel. No: we are confronted here with something opposed to the reign of life that the Lord proclaimed; with something, therefore, that a Christian must reject. Neither is it possible to limit the idea of "the poor" to a particular social class. Any interpretation of poverty that reduces the poor and the option for the poor to the purely economic and political level is therefore mistaken and can claim no support from our thinking.

The life of the poor is, in practice, a state of hunger and exploitation, insufficient health care, lack of decent housing, difficult access to schooling, low wages and unemployment, struggle for rights, and oppression. But that is not all. To be poor is also a way of feeling, knowing, reasoning, making friends, loving, believing, suffering, celebrating, and praying. In other words, the poor form a world. Commitment to the poor means entering into their universe (or in some cases remaining in it but now with a clearer awareness) and living in it. It means regarding it no longer as a place of work but as a place of residence. It means not going into this world for a few hours in order to bear witness to the gospel, but rather emerging from it each morning to proclaim the good news to every human being.

We are convinced that there is no Christian life without songs to God, without thanksgiving for God's love, without prayer. But the song is sung by individuals in particular historical situations.

In the Latin American setting we may ask: How are we to thank God for the gift of life in a situation that bears the stamp of premature and unjust death? There are no easy answers to this question. It is certain, however, that, as the lives of the poor prove, such a situation does not do away with songs of thanksgiving; it does not silence the voice of the poor. It can even be said that Latin America is living in a time of judgment, a propitious moment, a *kairos*, a call to set out on new ways in fidelity to the Lord.

Theology and the Social Sciences

Theology always makes use of one or another kind of rationality, although it is not identified with it. The rationality corresponds at any given moment to the cultural universe in which believers are living. Every theology inquires into the meaning of God's word for us at the present historical moment, and any attempted answers are in the context of our culture and of the problems which the people of our time are facing. In response to this cultural universe the church is constantly reformulating the gospel message for our contemporaries and for ourselves. Human knowledge today, as we are aware, is extremely complex and pluridimensional: philosophy, the sciences, forms of artistic expression. All these must play a part in the work of understanding the faith.

Talk of present-day poverty in Latin America leads to an effort to know it both descriptively and by determination of its causes. This determination is effected through analyses and interpretations in the area of the social sciences. The episcopal documents at Medellín and Puebla, as well as other episcopal documents, have been engaged in precisely that kind of determination.

In today's social sciences there are certain elements that come from Marxist analysis. This fact, however, does not in any way justify an identification of the social sciences with Marxist analysis, especially if we take into account what Father Arrupe called "the exclusive character" of Marxist analysis ("Letter on Marxist Analysis," December, 1980, no. 6). It follows that the appeal to the social sciences in the theology of liberation has for its primary purpose to promote a better understanding of the social reality of the Latin American people (the reality in which, as a matter of historical fact, many are living out their faith and hope). On the other hand, recourse by theologians to the social sciences, or other branches of human knowledge, necessarily implies what the Instruction calls "a critical examination of the analytical methods borrowed from other disciplines" (VII, 10; see also section IX; Puebla, no. 524; Document of the Peruvian Bishops, no. 36).

A Theocentric Option

The "scandal of the cross" sheds light on the situation of unjust death in which so many in Latin America are living. It does so by sharpening the contrast between this situation of death and the gift of life in Christ. In the dramatic account of the trial of Jesus in the gospel of John, we see him passing gradually from the role of defendant to that of judge (see John 18–19). In Johannine theology the cross thus becomes a throne for this "man" who is identified with the poor of this world (see Mt. 25:31–46) but who at the same time is a king. He is the king of a kingdom of life, and it is precisely his proclamation of life that brings him to persecution and death on the cross. The reality of this kingdom is confirmed by the Father who bestows victory over death in the resurrection of Jesus.

It is in the light of this life that comes through death that we must assess the situation of premature and unjust death in which the great majority are living in Latin America. The assessment will make clear to us that the deeper meaning of what we call "integral liberation" (a theme present in liberation theology from its beginnings) is, in the final analysis, the acceptance of the kingdom of life. In this context, "life" includes all dimensions of the human, in keeping with the all-embracing will of God; it is therefore contrary to the situation of unjust death in which the poor and oppressed are living. It is contrary to the state of affairs that Medellín and Puebla described as being, from the theological point of view, a "sinful situation."

For this reason, because the gift of life leads us to reject unjust death, the ultimate motive at work in what is called "the preferential option for the poor" is to be found in the God in whom we believe. There can be other worthwhile motives: the emergence of the poor in our time, the social analysis of their situation, human compassion, acknowledgment of the poor as agents of their own history. But, to tell the truth, for Christians the basis of this commitment is theocentric. Solidarity with the poor and the oppressed is based on our faith in God, the God of life who is revealed in Jesus Christ.

BEARING WITNESS TO THE RESURRECTION

Proclaiming the Gospel of Jesus Christ

The realization that the Lord loves us and the acceptance of the unmerited gift of the Lord's love are the deepest source of the joy of those who live by God's word. Evangelization is the communication or sharing of this joy. It is the sharing of the good news of God's love that has changed our lives. The proclamation is in a sense free and unmerited, just as is the love that is the source of our proclamation.

The point of departure for the work of evangelization is thus always an experience of the Lord: an experience of the Father's love that makes us his sons and daughters, and transforms us by making us more fully the brothers and sisters of all human beings. To proclaim the gospel is to proclaim the mystery of divine rebirth and fellowship: a mystery hidden through all the ages and revealed now in the dead and risen Christ. For this reason, to proclaim the gospel is to call men and women into an *ecclesia*; it is to gather them into a community. Only in a community can faith be lived out in love; only there can it be celebrated and deepened; only there can it be experienced as simultaneously fidelity to the Lord and solidarity with all human beings.

When we accept the divine message, we are converted to the Other in others. It is with them that we live out the message. Faith cannot be lived in pure privacy within the self; it is the negation of every turning in upon the self.

The mission the risen Lord gives his disciples in Galilee, where he himself had preached, is to make disciples of all nations (see Mt. 28:19). The universal message thus bears the mark of the forgotten and despised land of Galilee. The God proclaimed by Jesus Christ is a God whose call is universal and addressed to every human being; at the same time, however, God has a preferential love for the poor and dispossessed. Universality is not only not opposed to this predilection (which is not to be mistaken for exclusivity) but even requires it in order to make clear the meaning of the universality itself. The preference, in turn, has its proper setting in the call that God addresses to every human being.

The twofold requirement of universality and preferential love is a challenge to the community of the Lord's disciples. This community is the express and authentic locus of what John XXIII called the "church of the poor," for it is the vocation of the entire church to be a church of the poor. This point has been emphasized ever since, by Medellín, Puebla, and John Paul II (see also the 1984 Instruction, IX, 9). The dynamism at work in the proclamation of the good news (which reveals to us that we are God's children, and brothers and sisters to one another) leads to the creation of a community, the church, which will be a visible sign to all of liberation in Christ.

Three dimensions or levels may be distinguished in the process of liberation: liberation of a social, political, cultural, and economic kind; specifically human liberation with its various aspects; and liberation from sin. In the final analysis, the process is single but not monolithic; various dimensions, aspects, or levels must be distinguished and not confused with one another. Neither separation nor confusion, neither verticalism nor horizontalism (see Puebla, nos. 321–29).

Only in this way is it possible to preserve both the unity that the free and unmerited initiative of God has bestowed on every area of human history, and the relative autonomies without which the coherence of human action and the gratuitousness of grace cannot be asserted with sufficient clarity. I refer to this as a "Chalcedonian principle" because it is inspired by the great statement of christological dogma at Chalcedon: unity without confusion, distinction without separation. The end result is what liberation theology speaks of as total liberation in Christ.

Kingdom and Liberation

Liberation is at bottom a gift of the Lord. St. Paul tells us that "for freedom Christ has set us free" (Gal. 5:1). This means liberation from sin, which is a self-centered turning in upon oneself. Sin is in effect a refusal to love others and, consequently, a refusal to love the Lord. According to the Bible, sin, or the breaking off of friendship with God and others, is the ultimate cause of the want, injustice, and oppression in which human beings live (see Medellín, *Justice*, no. 3).

The claim that sin is the ultimate cause is in no way a denial that these situations have structural causes and are objectively conditioned. The point is rather to stress that things do not happen by chance, and that behind an unjust structure there is a responsible individual or collective will, a will to reject God and others. It must also be kept in mind that no social transformation, however radical, automatically brings with it the suppression of all ills (see Medellín, *Justice*, no. 3, and the 1984 Instruction, XI, 9).

Thomas Aquinas distinguishes between "freedom from" and "freedom for." The first refers to freedom from sin, selfishness, injustice, need, and situations calling for deliverance. The second refers to the purpose of the first freedom—namely, love and communion; this is the final phase of liberation. "Free to love": this formula, which is inspired by St. Paul and St. Augustine, brings out the full meaning of the process of liberation to which many Latin American Christians are committed. In the final analysis, to set free means to give life, and life signifies communion with God and others. Puebla speaks of liberation for communion and participation.

And in fact, by giving us his Spirit, Christ brings us into communion with God and all human beings. More specifically: by bringing us into this communion and launching us upon a quest for complete communion, the Spirit overcomes sin, which is the denial of love, and all the consequences of sin.

From this it follows that the coming of the kingdom cannot be identified with the historical embodiments of human liberation. The growth of the kingdom is indeed a process that takes place in history through liberation, to the extent that liberation means an important fulfillment of the human person and is a condition for a new and fraternal society. But the growth of the kingdom entails more than that. To the extent that the kingdom takes shape in historical actions leading to liberation, it also reveals the limits and ambiguities of these embodiments, points forward to its complete fulfillment, and effectively urges human beings on to total communion. There is, then, no identification.

Without the liberating events of history, the kingdom does not grow, but the process of liberation only destroys the roots of oppression and of the exploitation of one human being by another; this is not the same thing as the coming of the kingdom, which is first and foremost a gift. It can even be said that historical, political, liberating actions mean the growth of the kingdom and are saving events; they are not, however, the coming of the kingdom, they do not represent complete salvation. They are historical embodiments of the kingdom and by that very fact also pointers toward the fulness of the kingdom; there precisely is the difference (see the Document of the Peruvian Episcopal Conference on Liberation Theology, nos. 50–53).

A Twofold Approach

From the viewpoint of theological reflection, the challenge we face in Latin America is to find a language about God that grows out of the situation created by the unjust poverty in which the broad masses live (despised races, exploited social classes, marginalized cultures, discrimination against women). This language must at the same time be fed by the hope that heartens a people in search of its liberation. It is in this context of sufferings and joys, uncertainties and certainties, generous commitments and ambiguities, that our understanding of the faith must be continually renewed.

It can be said, I think, that a prophetic language and a mystical language are being born in this soil of exploitation and hope. The problem here, as in the Book of Job, is to speak of God in the context of the suffering of the innocent. The language of contemplation acknowledges that everything has its origin in the Father's unmerited love. The language of prophecy denounces the situation of injustice and exploitation in which the peoples of Latin America are living, and denounces as well the structural causes of this situation. Puebla tells us that we must learn to recognize "the suffering features of Christ the Lord" in faces scarred by the suffering of an oppressed people (nos. 31–39).

Without prophecy, the language of contemplation runs the risk of detachment from the history in which God is acting and in which we encounter God. Without the mystical dimension, the language of prophecy can narrow its vision and weaken its perception of that which makes all things new. "Sing to the Lord; praise the Lord! For he has delivered the life of the needy from the hand of evildoers" (Jer. 20:13).

To sing and to set free; thanksgiving and demand for justice. Christian existence unfolds between the freely given gift and the demand. At the source and, as it were, holding everything in its embrace, is the free and unmerited love of God. But this gift calls for behavior in the form of works of love for one's neighbor and especially for the most helpless. Here we have the challenge facing a Christian life that seeks to avoid all possible spiritualist evasions and all possible political reductionisms and to be faithful to the God of Jesus Christ.

The aim of these two languages is to communicate the gift of God's reign as revealed in the life, death, and resurrection of Jesus. This is the heart of the message we are now rediscovering in the setting of our own real world. It calls us together as a community, a church, within which we attempt to think our faith. Theology is an ecclesial function. It is done in a church that has the obligation of bearing witness in history to a life that is victorious over death. Being a witness to the resurrection means choosing life and indeed all expressions of life, because nothing is outside the comprehensive embrace of God's reign.

This witness to life (life material and spiritual, individual and social, present and future) is particularly important in a continent marked by premature and unjust death; it is also particularly important in efforts to achieve liberation from oppression. The existence of such death and of sin is a denial of the resurrection. Witnesses to the resurrection can therefore join scripture in asking the ironic question: "Death, where is your victory?" That is the question suggested by a testimony like that of Archbishop Romero, to name but one among many.

We celebrate this life in the eucharist, the action that is the primary work of the ecclesial community. When we share the bread we commemorate the love and fidelity that brought Jesus to his death, as well as the resurrection that put the seal of approval on his mission to the poor. The breaking of bread is at once the point of departure and the point of arrival of the Christian community. In the breaking of bread the community expresses its radical sharing of the human suffering that is caused in many instances by the lack of bread; it also joyfully acknowledges the presence of the risen Lord who gives life and sustains the hope of the people whom his actions and word have called together.

The aim of the theology of liberation is to be a language about God, and to be this in the communion of the church. It is an effort to make the word of life present in a world of oppression, injustice, and death.

THE DISCUSSION

Gérard Defois: We are gathered here for a university function. It is a great joy for me now to welcome Gustavo Gutiérrez, an alumnus of our faculty of theology. After his philosophical studies Gustavo discovered, while among us, the meaning of theology, and today he shows his friendship for us by presenting his dissertation in theology, a dissertation in the form of his various published works.

Gustavo, we look forward with pleasure to the fruit of your reflections, hoping to learn from you how universal our evangelical responsibilities are. In other words, we hope to learn from you what the Spirit is saying to the church, as the Book of Revelation puts it. Your thinking will, I am sure, be a light for our feet on the paths of Christian solidarity and fidelity.

Now it is Gustavo Gutiérrez's turn to speak for the works that he has published and that we have accepted as a dissertation for a doctorate in theology.

Gustavo Gutiérrez: I am grateful for Msgr. Defois' words, and I hope they will set the tone for this dialogue. I am presenting a body of scientific theological work that has been done in an ecclesial spirit. Theology is an ecclesial function; it is reflection, done as seriously as possible, in the service of the proclamation of the gospel.

Henri Bourgeois: Let us then begin a discussion of your various works on the basis of the presentation you have completed. The first participant will be Christian Duquoc, director of your dissertation.

Christian Duquoc: Dear Gustavo, I find it a bit awkward playing the university game in view of the longstanding friendship between us. On the other hand, I must say I am very glad of this meeting, for personal as well as ecclesial reasons. This is because for many years now the theologians of the Third World have wanted a real dialogue with their European colleagues, and in my opinion a purely friendly dialogue is not enough. The best thing in the circumstances would be a critical examination that can claim to be "official," and today provides an occasion for precisely that. This faculty of theology is part of a Catholic university, whose chancellor is Cardinal A. Decourtray. The doctorate will therefore be a recognition of your theological endeavors, and you will receive an official title because of them. But such a step requires not only documents but a genuine theological discussion of them. It is up to me to begin this discussion.

What has very much impressed me, both personally and as a European theologian, about the work that has led you to the doctorate is what you said this morning with such eloquence and depth. I think that your theology, which I have read extensively, has always been an evangelical challenge to me. In reading what you have written, I find myself, I believe, in the very place where conversion occurs in the church that speaks to me as a theologian. In all honesty I may say that rarely have I come upon works that, like yours, raise so many personal questions.

I must enter now into the university game, but before formulating any questions I should like to point out what I regard as fundamental in the theology that has arisen in Latin America and especially in your own theology. I mean that the viewpoint you have adopted for reflecting on the Christian faith—the viewpoint of the poor—is not a romantic but a structural viewpoint. For that reason it is doubly real and demanding, as you said again this morning in your doctoral lecture.

First of all, this viewpoint brings to light the rupture hidden in the success of a society like the European. I think that perhaps the most important lesson you taught me as I listened to you this morning is that the success of Western society, of European society, has had evil effects. The theology being done in Latin

America has shown the extent to which Western theology has failed to take into account these evil effects of a success.

The second important thing, from the viewpoint of revelation, is the urgent demands you set before us. Your theology uses two paradigms: the paradigm of the exodus and the paradigm of the cross. Under the first you speak of a people that becomes conscious of itself because it is delivered from slavery and is established as a people by liberating itself or being liberated. The second paradigm, that of the cross, may seem in some respects to be contrary to the first, because it says that God, in the Son Jesus, becomes a slave and is crucified outside the city. In fact, liberated slaves who developed a genuine consciousness of being a people lead to the condemned slave.

The originality of this theology seems to me to consist in this: it is rooted in a Christian praxis that endeavors to think the faith from the standpoint of a humiliated race—the Amerindians, the marginalized, women, the hopeless—and to turn them, in the light of the double paradigm of the exodus and the cross, into a people of hope. This means an attempt to open up a space in which hopelessness disappears. You moved me especially when you reminded us that the God of our faith is a God of life who rejects every form of death.

In my opinion, these two paradigms have led in your theology to a kind of vital reading of what Christianity is. One might point out, for example, that in the theological summary you set before us, there is as it were a renewal of the overall reading of the Christian phenomenon. But this reading is not effected by abandoning entire parts of the Christian message, as was done in liberal theology under the pretext of adapting the message to the modern mind. No, this is something completely different. The issue here is to show the transforming power of hope, a virtue that has all too often been given a place only in speculation. This morning made me really aware of the importance you give to the ancient Christian assertion of the resurrection in terms of an entire people's hope of life. I greatly appreciate your determination to keep our Christian identity clear.

The questions I should like to raise are the following, now that the time has come to enter into the university game. The questions arise out of some presuppositions that especially impressed me, perhaps for reasons not connected solely with the theology of liberation. My attention has also been caught by some references to the Jewish people and their theology, which I see you making in connection with the Book of Job. The same point also impressed me quite a bit in your lecture, for I believe that what you are concerned with in the Book of Job is the relation between the God of history and the God of the Bible.

These, then, are my questions. The first is in reference to what you say in your *A Theology of Liberation* (pp. 153ff.) about the unity of history: "History Is One." You say that "there is only one human destiny, irreversibly assumed by Christ, the Lord of history. . . . Although there may be different approaches to understanding it . . . the fundamental affirmation is clear: there is only one history—a 'Christo-finalized' history" (p. 153).

If we adopt the viewpoint of faith, we can only agree with you; contemporary theology is now clear on this point. But as soon as we try to relate the claim to experience, the difficulty begins, because we find sets of tools being used that are in the final analysis incompatible with one another. My question, then, is: What set of instruments am I to use in order to show this unity, in this century and in light of our present experience, that is, in a world that you said, a few hours ago, is characterized by the unjust suffering of the innocent?

Gustavo Gutiérrez: I should like, first, to express my satisfaction with the kind of dialogue we are about to engage in for the sake of this academic function. I am also happy to be here with this beloved faculty. As I said this morning, I expect to find this dialogue very profitable. I wish to submit some theological reflections to your judgment.

I am obliged to you for the question about the unity of history, for this is a central and frequently occurring theme in contemporary theology, as you said. I think that it is theologically possible to speak of history as one, provided always that at the same time one makes distinctions, as I do, within this history. I could repeat of history what I said of liberation: it is not monolithic, but it is profoundly one. I confess that in my own case this theological idea comes from the time when I was a student here and had occasion to work with some friends on a subject that was very important during those years: the question of the natural and the supernatural. I derived great profit from the discussions of Henri de Lubac's book, *Le surnaturel*, Rahner's idea of the "supernatural existential," and Blondel's "transnatural." From the debate I concluded that the critique to which Father de Lubac, following in the steps of others, had subjected the idea of a pure nature, marked the end of one phase of the subject. It was also clear that the question needed to be approached not in terms of abstract notions of nature and supernature but from the historical, Augustinian viewpoint, as Father de Lubac said. Along the same line, Rahner brought clarity to the somewhat vague terms used by de Lubac and maintained that we are in the presence, concretely, of a unitary human being who bears the stamp of grace (Rahner's "supernatural existential").

Against this background it can be said that in the final analysis history is one—that is, that every human life is ultimately a yes or no to God, to God's offer of grace. When I say "ultimately" I am saying "radically." Clearly, this does not mean I am denying the necessity of making distinctions and of trying to determine—no easy task—the limits of what we call "natural." At that time this was a much discussed matter. Human actions are complex; they have aspects that are from nature and aspects due to the presence of grace. How are we to separate them out? But—and I repeat the point—this difficulty does not, in my opinion, eliminate distinctions.

If we adopt the historical and concrete point of view, we see human existence as unitary, and yet distinctions must be made within it if we are to understand it. Otherwise, the gratuitous aspect of grace—if you will permit me the redundancy—gets lost. It has always been difficult to find an accurate terminology for speaking of so complex a reality. During my studies here, and later on when I was following the Roman courses of Father Juan Alfaro, a great specialist in this area, I had occasion to spend time on the subject; all that helped me to realize the complexity and difficulty of the theme. I have always tried to make clear both the unity and the distinctions. I am put off by any interpretation that confuses the levels.

But you have asked me a much more difficult question: What set of tools are we to use in order to express this unity today?

There is nevertheless a narrow track, and I shall describe it. Both my faith and my theology make me believe firmly in these distinctions, which are important for understanding the aspect which, as I said, seems to me fundamental in Christian revelation: the gratuitousness of God's love.

On the other hand, contact with my people has shown me that they are a people at once Christian and oppressed. I do not claim that they are all very good Christians—although there are such among them—but simply that they are religious and think of themselves as Christians. At the same time, they are an oppressed people who are denied the most elementary human rights. All this means that their faith is marked by the exploitation and marginalization that they experience, and that their experience of oppression bears the stamp of their Christianity. These two dimensions exist in the daily life of this people; they exist, that is, within a concrete unity in which it is impossible to separate them.

The distinctions are important, but we must remember that the Lord, like the sower in the gospel, rises very early, before the theologians make distinctions. In historical terms, there is a unity that causes the poor to live and react both as oppressed human beings and as Christians to various situations. The question was: "What set of tools is to be used?" I believe I have no other tool than my personal and pastoral experience. That is perhaps not the best answer, but I confess that it is my contact with that people which enables me to see better both the unity and the distinctions of which I have spoken.

Christian Duquoc: My second question has to do with a point I touched on earlier in connection with the success of European society and its consequences in other parts of the world. The question is this: Do you think that, speaking from the viewpoint of history, liberation theology has a different point of departure than modern theology?

Gustavo Gutiérrez: I think it does. We must go back to certain situations in order to understand the differences between the two theologies. The principal partner in the dialogue of modern Western theology has been unbelievers or else believers affected by unbelief and the criticisms of the Enlightenment. In the theology of liberation, on the other hand, our principal interlocutor has been nonpersons insofar as they are considered as nonpersons.

The question that Dietrich Bonhoeffer asked in the first of these two contexts is: How are we to speak of God in a world come of age? In answering this question, theologians frequently fail to take into account that persons are the new and dominant subjects in the human race, and that this fact has given rise to a subproduct—namely, nonpersons, the poor of today. I ask whether a critique (including the theological aspect) to be made of this theology as it legitimately tries to answer the questions of the modern mind, would not be that it fails to look at more than one side of history. For, on the other side, which we call the underside of history, we have the creation of new forms of oppression. The oppression of human beings certainly did not begin with the modern period, but in that period it has taken on a new modality. And the moderns who pose questions to the faith—questions that a sizable part of contemporary theology is trying to answer—belong to social groups, cultures, and countries that have been creating new forms of domination.

For this reason it would be a mistake simply to juxtapose these two theological perspectives. I mean it would be a mistake to suppose that a theology arising from the nonperson, the poor, has nothing to say to a theology that starts with the questions asked by the modern mind. I think that, on the contrary, those speaking from the underside of history do have something to say to the theology that has hitherto been the prevailing and most important theology in the Christian churches. The question: How are we to tell nonpersons, the poor and oppressed, that God is their Father? has its source in the least of the human race, in those who until now have been regarded as absent from history.

It seems to me that one criticism must be made of Bonhoeffer (though allowance must also be made for the fact that his beautiful last book consists of notes and is not a finished product). One thing cries out for attention: the fact that when he speaks of a world come of age he never refers to the underside of this world. (There is indeed an allusion in one short text in which he gives an overview of ten years and says that it is necessary to look at the history of the human race "from beneath." It is a fine passage, but it does not reach the point of becoming a new perspective.) The result is that in his work the "world come of age" is the modern world; this is clear from his descriptions of the rise of the modern mind. I believe that a large part of European theology thinks the only human questions are the questions posed by the modern (and European) mentality.

I wonder whether, when it is said the church ought to be present in the world, many do not understand "world" to mean exclusively the modern world and its challenges. But the human scene includes more than that; there are "nonmodern" areas that pose challenges to the faith and in addition are a source of life and theological reflection for the church. These areas (the majority of the human race!) make up the underside of history.

Christian Duquoc: My third question is a more personal one that I ask as I read *A Theology of Liberation* but that comes to me out of my European context. Our age (I speak very schematically) has been characterized by the fact that technoscience has produced what might be called a form of religious indifference. As a result, Christianity is viewed as one opinion among others and as having no more content than the others.

I have often had the impression, well grounded or not, that those working in the theology of liberation have underestimated the power of technoscience to secularize. I ask myself what the effect will be on deeply religious peoples if there is a massive cultural, technological, and scientific importation of what in Europe has produced a kind of secularistic radicalism among the young. I myself do not know the answer, and therefore I ask you: Do you think that this impact of technoscience is linked at bottom with a phase of European history that has been shaped by a series of mainly ideological factors, and that the same effect will not follow in a different historical setting? Do you think that the liberation perspective of the Christian communities of Latin America, together with the theological reflection that is its second act, can help development to take a different course there?

Gustavo Gutiérrez: My previous answers have, I think, been a little too long; I shall therefore try to respond more briefly.

I do not feel that I am in a position to give a categorical answer to your questions. The point you raise is one that we have discussed a great deal in Latin America. I think that science and technology do in fact have a secularizing effect, as has been seen in Europe. But I also think that historical phenomena do not repeat themselves in precisely the same form, despite what is usually said about history.

In my opinion, we will have in Latin America, and are already beginning to have, a kind of secularization, but it is occurring within a complex history influenced by our culture and also by the present-day action of the church. In the final analysis, history is not a matter of inevitable fate but depends in large part on our initiatives and actions. I think that we in Latin America can learn a lesson from the European experience of secularization and its consequences, and will be able to confront our greatest present problem: poverty. It is my own conviction that if we are able to be present to this poverty as Christians, the consequences that secularization has had in Europe will not be repeated. This will depend a great deal, of course, on what we are capable of accomplishing today.

These matters were much discussed before Puebla. The question (I too am speaking sketchily) was this: What is the major pastoral problem that the church faces: poverty or secularization? Some of us answer that the major problem is poverty, this being the overall situation of the majority of the Latin American population, and that by confronting it we will be choosing the best way of responding to the challenges that secularization presents to the faith. (This was the perspective adopted at Puebla.)

This depends, admittedly, on the course our history takes. I do not want to be dramatic, but I think that if the church and we Latin American Christians do not respond to the great problems facing persons on this continent, the result may be something like what has occurred in Europe (I do not deny that secularization has also yielded some positive values). But, to repeat, the outcome depends partially on us. It depends on how we, as a church, face the challenges of the present.

For the same reason, I think that the liberation perspective adopted by the Christian communities, and indeed by the church as a whole since Medellín and Puebla, has an important role to play. That is also the wager we are making in the theology of liberation.

In conclusion, I should like to express my full agreement with what you have called the paradigms of the exodus and the cross. I think that the two are truly central in the theological writings I have attempted. In addition, both have great importance in and for the life of the Latin American poor.

Vincent Cosmao: When Henri Bourgeois, our Dean, wrote asking me to be a member of the jury, I felt that my only valid reason for accepting was what I had witnessed in the past. For, between 1967 and 1972, I worked in Rome on the Pontifical Commission for Justice and Peace. In 1969 we organized, in collaboration with the World Council of Churches, a theological conference of the "Theology of Development." If I am not mistaken, this was the first time anything was said in Europe about the "theology of liberation"; it was said in a position paper of Gustavo Gutiérrez.

I come to my first question. If we turn to the social analysis that lies behind, if not at the origin of, the theology of liberation, we find (I believe all are in agreement on this point) the theory of dependence or rather the social, cultural, and intellectual effects that the theory of dependence had on the collective Latin American consciousness and more particularly on the collective Christian consciousness there.

The theory of dependence was an important phase in worldwide reflection on what we were still calling "development." We may use the name without falling into the "developmentalism" that you rightly rejected and from which we too very quickly tried to free ourselves, although by other ways than yours. Putting the matter very schematically, I would say that worldwide reflection on underdevelopment has gone through three phases, which at the same time constitute three levels of our collective consciousness.

In a first phase, development was conceived solely in terms of the transfer of technology, for the supposition was that underdevelopment was to be explained as entirely the fault of technological backwardness.

In a second phase, development was thought of rather in terms of transforming the system that had produced the underdevelopment; in this approach, underdevelopment was a direct or indirect effect of, a phase produced by, the new international economic order.

My impression is that you held aloof from this thinking because you regarded this new international economic order as a new snare being set by imperialism. I confess that I was one of those who in 1973 believed that something would change in the Third World because of the power the oil business was giving to some countries. Nothing happened, but it seems to me that the problem was not therefore badly posed from the political standpoint.

Well, even though nothing happened at the countless international conferences that talked of a new international economic order, one fine day even the industrialized countries became aware that something was indeed going on in the so-called "underdeveloped" countries. What was happening was that the poorest of the poor, those who had nothing to sell in the marketplace and were stripped of everything, had taken a stand and had decided to become the subjects, the agents, of what we were still calling their development.

I think that as you in Latin America have pursued your sociological and theological journey, you have found a way of skipping the second stage or phase. From a refutation of the analysis of underdevelopment as due to technological backwardness and from a vision of development as a matter of the transfer of technology, you passed directly, in a way, to the assertion or verification of what I would call the resurrection of subjects or agents. It was in this sense that you said, even at that time, that only the poor as classes or peoples can be the subjects of their own history.

My question, therefore, is this: From a focus on the liberation of the oppressed, have you not passed theologically, and should you not pass in your social analysis as well, to a focus on resurrection? It can be shown, it seems to me, that for some years now, your point of reference has been less the exodus than Easter, and that the main axis of your discourse is now the victory of life over death. Have you not begun in your work a theology of resurrection?

Gustavo Gutiérrez: At the end, your question turned into a very theological one. Earlier, however, you touched on some points regarding the theory of dependence, and I should like to begin by saying something about them.

In the 1960s the "theory of dependence" was an important contribution of the social sciences in Latin America. There were those in Latin America who were trying to understand the causes of the underdevelopment to which you referred a moment ago. They spoke at that time of the dependence of our countries on others, and this helped a great deal in understanding our situation.

Though I am approaching the situation at a theological level, I want to remind you that the theory of dependence was important to us in the social field—that is, in understanding the social reality of the poor and the causes of the intolerably unjust situation in which they live. For, if we take the poor seriously, we must understand their situation. It is not enough to say that the poor exist and that their poverty is very great; it is also necessary to try to understand the reasons for this poverty, its causes.

In this effort to grasp social reality, we were using a tool that we theologians had not developed ourselves—namely, the social sciences—and, very concretely, a Latin American contribution to the social sciences: the theory of dependence. That is what theology has always done: it has accepted from the current age a tool for understanding a specific reality that it then reflected on theologically with the help of its own proper methods.

As I turn now to the main point of your question, allow me a brief observation with regard to the exodus. The theme of the exodus has been and still is an important one for us, but I think it an overstatement to say that it was the major theme in our theology of liberation. It is important to us because the exodus has been the basic historical experience of the Jewish people and has set its mark on the entire Bible. But I think that we have also treated other themes as important. From the outset, other aspects have been essential in our view—for example, poverty according to the Bible; this is a subject on which greater effort has been spent (including many pages in my own writings) than on the theme of the exodus.

You are correct, however, when you say that the question of life and death has become increasingly important to us. That is certainly the case. We are now more conscious than before that a theology of liberation is, in a sense, a theology of life confronted with a reality full of death: physical and cultural death, but also death in the Pauline sense, since sin is also a death. And when you say that liberation theology is increasingly a theology of resurrection, I can only say that I agree with you. The theme of resurrection was, of course, present previously, since it is unavoidable in a work of theology; but I think that as a matter of fact we are today more perceptive and sensitive to its meaning. There has been an evolution in this area; our theology is increasingly a theology of life, of resurrection. Father Duquoc said a few minutes ago, and I agree, that daily contact with death, with different kinds of death, compels us to emphasize long familiar aspects of our common faith. But I also repeat my agreement with what Father Duquoc said about the central presence of the paradigms of the exodus and the cross in liberation theology. ·

Vincent Cosmao: The second question I want to ask refers to sin, for I have the impression that this is a point on which there is at present some lack of movement. The sin of the world, the world of sin, the world structured by sin: Where in the concept of sin is the point at which you pass from social analysis to theological reflection? And in order to determine this point, would it not be necessary to look at what sin essentially is: an opposition to God, and therefore to locate sin at the root of the contradictions we presently find in a world that produces poverty, want, and death?

Gustavo Gutiérrez: I think I can offer some remarks on this truly central question. First of all, when we began the "theology of liberation" seventeen years ago, other theological endeavors were underway which some might have thought of as close to ours. There was a theology of progress; some years earlier, there had been talk of a theology of earthly realities; there was also a theology of development.

These currents of thought seemed to us to be always a bit overoptimistic with regard to history, and so we kept a certain distance from them. Sin was not an important subject in these theologies. According to them, the human race was advancing toward its destiny, and everything was going well. They also felt that the church had talked too much of sin and had fallen behind the advances of history. It was necessary (they said) to take seriously the fact that Christendom was dead. Something of this was to be found in Teilhard de Chardin. I think too—and I say this with all respect—that the description in the introduction to Vatican II's Constitution on the Church in the Modern World is tinged by that optimism. The more critical observations on the contemporary world came, as we know, from those who at the time were known as the conciliar minority.

Now, in countries like ours we cannot fail to see the negative aspects of the modern world. The concern among us is not simply with being open to contemporary thought or to contemporary science and technology. My people have elementary needs: food, medicine, shelter, education. It is impossible, therefore, that we should not be aware of the effects that this situation of poverty and death is having in today's world. Therefore, too, sin has an important place in the theology of liberation. It has been present from the beginning. In the opening pages of my book, *A Theology of Liberation*, I speak of what we call the third level of liberation: liberation from sin, and the resultant communion with God and with other human beings.

This brings me to my second remark. Although I said it before, I am glad to emphasize the point here again: in the perspective proper to liberation theology, we insist that in the final analysis the root of social injustice is the rejection of love—that is, sin—which you quite rightly call "opposition to God." I think that this has always been important in our minds. In the early books on liberation theology we emphasized the social dimensions of sin, because at that time, despite estimable studies of sin in the Bible, these dimensions did not receive much attention, whereas the personal aspects of sin were always present. Today the emphasis has perhaps changed and suggests the need of a new balance. Some persons think so, and I believe they are correct.

The important thing, nonetheless, was and is sensitivity to sin (the breaking of friendship with God and other human beings), a sensitivity awakened by the situation of poverty and social injustice of which the Medellín Conference spoke. It called the Latin American situation a "sinful situation"; despite the scandal that that assertion caused in some individuals, Puebla repeated it eleven years later. In fact, what Medellín said only once, Puebla repeated at least ten times. One thing that contributed to this stress was the addresses of John Paul II during the Puebla Conference, for in these addresses the social aspect of sin is heavily underscored. Emphases may vary; the important thing is to know how to maintain "the whole message of salvation," as the 1984 Instruction says (XI, 16; see also Puebla, no. 338).

Vincent Cosmao: Christian Duquoc's final question suggests another to me: May we not think that technoscience will eventually lead to secularization among you as well? Is not the thing that threatens and oppresses your peoples an idolatry, a sacralization of the very system that exploits them?

Gustavo Gutiérrez: In present-day Latin America we are, I think, increasingly conscious of this situation. Your question is also a very biblical one, for in the Bible the rejection of God takes the form above all of idolatry, and that is what we are seeing in Latin America. In these circumstances, such expressions as the "service of Mammon," as opposed, in the gospel, to the service of God, have a very weighty and concrete meaning for us.

When St. Paul says on two occasions that greed is a form of idolatry, we in Latin America feel his words to be cruelly applicable. Idolatry consists precisely in giving oneself to someone or something other than God and making it the unqualified reference point of our lives. I think that among us power, money, and so on are forms of idolatry, even in individuals who claim (whether honestly or not, God alone knows) to believe in God. I think the question of idolatry has acquired a new meaning among us, even though the problem is a very ancient one, more ancient even than atheism. It is a subject to which we are giving increasing attention.

Bernard Sesboüé: At the beginning of my participation I would like to utter two words: seriousness and respect. Seriousness in face of the tragic situation of an entire continent, a situation we rich Europeans have great difficulty in grasping. Respect for all the peoples whose basic human rights are being violated and who face premature death; respect for all those who carry on the struggle of love for the poor and set their own lives at risk;

respect humbler still for the martyrs of these ordeals. When I think of Archbishop Romero, for example, I cannot help remembering here Father Yves de Montcheuil, a renowned French theologian who was executed on the firing range at Grenoble on August 10, 1944.

The things at stake for entire peoples and their churches can make our academic discussion today seem unimportant. I myself do not think that it is in fact unimportant. I think of this defense of a dissertation as an occasion for a penetrating and constructive dialogue between the Latin American theology of liberation and European theology. I am convinced that we have much to contribute to each other and that we can thus serve to promote a better relation between intention and concept, to use the language of Kant. Let me explain: what I read and understand to be at work in liberation theology is the intention or quest of a new *status confessionis*, that is, the emergence of a datum so fundamental for the confession of faith that the decision one makes in regard to it will become a decision for or against the faith. Indeed, has not the promotion of justice perhaps become a problem of faith in our day? This is something that we especially must understand, we who belong to the rich and developed countries.

As I follow your writings with this in mind, I seem to see an increasing insertion of theological elements that eliminate the unilateralism I thought I saw in your initial positions. Many of my questions have been answered by your recent writings. I have also noted, however, the repetition of certain theses that do not seem to me to have been given the theological justification, or the theological expression, that would grant them an indisputable permanence. In your writings you frequently make broad references to the spirituality of the Society of Jesus, to its validity, and to the teaching of Father Arrupe. This pleases me as a Jesuit, and for this reason my starting point in the considerations and questions I shall propose to you will be the attitude of "favorable prejudgment" of which the *Spiritual Exercises* speaks (no. 22). I shall endeavor in this way to be faithful to the spirit of Father Arrupe.

I should like to touch on two points, unconnected with one another, that roused my interest as I studied your writings. The first is the connection between liberation theology and justification by faith. The second is the distinction between duality and dualism as applied to the relation between human liberations and the coming of the kingdom.

Regarding the first point I have two questions: How do you understand the Pauline doctrine of justification by faith in your theological thinking on the praxis of liberation? What commentary would you offer, for example, on this sentence of yours: "Theology is a critical reflection based on the praxis of liberation and concerned with this praxis, in the light of the Lord's word as experienced and accepted in faith"? Secondly, What do you think of the necessity of applying a vocabulary derived from Marxist analysis?

Gustavo Gutiérrez: I should like to say first of all, and by way of a preliminary remark, that while authors can and must explain the meaning of their writings, they must also respect the opinion of those who have been good enough to read them. A reader may find things that an author does not intend, or thinks he does not intend, but which do not on that account fail to convey a part of the truth. The important thing is that a dialogue be started and that it be carried on with that "favorable prejudgment" that you have referred to as part of Ignatian spirituality and which we so much need in the church today. Would that we were all capable of it!

Your first question touches on an important point. In my first year of studies in this faculty, when we were studying the treatise on grace, I was greatly struck by the magnificent idea of the unmerited character of God's love and free initiative. This Pauline and Augustinian insight left its mark on my theological studies. I have endeavored, no doubt with imperfect success, to be faithful to this datum of biblical revelation in what I have written.

For reasons you will understand, I have recently had to do some rereading of my works, and I can tell you that the word "grace" (and its derivatives) is the one used most in *A Theology of Liberation.* I know that this claim may seem a purely quantitative one, but I think nonetheless that it is already a sign of something more.

My starting point in speaking of liberation has been to recall that it is not only liberation from forms of social oppression and from other limitations on a full human life but also liberation from sin. Liberation from sin—the ultimate root of all social injustice—is an unmerited gift of the Father in his Son made man. I consider this to be a key notion of that book. But I attempt also to underscore the importance of historical praxis, of the action of human beings in history. There is no contradiction between liberation from sin as an unmerited gift and human action in history. Acceptance of the gift of the kingdom calls for a certain behavior, for a commitment to other human beings, especially the poorest and most helpless. The saving action of God does not do away with human responsibility and the human task in history. Moreover, the history of Christian thought shows that passivity or quietism is not only not a real acknowledgment of the gratuitous love of God, but even denies or at least deforms it. Thomas Aquinas defined the proper relationship when he spoke, in Scholastic language, of first cause and second causes.

Nevertheless, the complexity of the subject is traditional and is not felt solely in the setting of liberation theology. The fundamentals to be preserved are clear: the action of God and the action of human beings. St. Augustine gave profound expression to their connection when he had God say: "I created you without you; I cannot save you without you." But this does not automatically do away with the risks of distortion in language and interpretation; these must always be kept in mind. You yourself mentioned, with an eye on liberation theology, that theology must be a critical reflection on historical praxis in the light of God's word accepted in faith. This critical judgment will keep historical praxis from replacing the gift of grace. The light of faith will be there to show that the starting point of everything is to be found in the divine initiative.

I think I may say that if there is anything I feel completely alien to me, it is any temptation to Pelagianism. My contact with St. Augustine from the beginning of my theological studies made that impossible. Furthermore, at no time in the church's history has the assertion of human freedom and creativity been taken to mean that human beings save themselves. Revelation itself emphasizes the value and dignity of the human being as created "in the image and likeness of God," from whom it received the commission to "subdue the earth." But the reference is to an activity and creativity that have their own proper sphere.

I had occasion recently to work on the beautiful Book of Job. This book and the Pauline letters are perhaps the biblical writings that show the keenest sense of salvation as the work of God alone. In any case, they are the writings that most fully ground this truth with arguments. I think that in them, and, of course, in the Bible as a whole, two approaches are taken to the mystery of God: gratuitousness and resultant obligation. The saving love of God is a gift, but its acceptance entails a commitment to one's neighbor. Christian life is located between the gratuitous gift and the obligation.

For this reason I think the idea of spiritual childhood is central to the gospel message. If we possess this outlook, we recognize God to be love and Father, and other human beings to be our brothers and sisters. The gift of filiation brings with it the obligation to create brotherly and sisterly relations among human beings. This idea — this relationship — is frequently brought up in my theological writings. But the fact that I make others my brothers and sisters does not give me any rights in relation to God. The obligation is to construct a human world; it does not empower me to make demands of God. Paul and the Book of Job, among others, have taught us this lesson in a definitive way. In *A Theology of Liberation* I try to bring out this point in a lengthy commentary on Matthew 25:31–46. In the 1960s this fundamental text of the gospel had a major and direct pastoral applicability among us. It inspired many beneficial commitments. Some persons, however, thought the passage to be saying that Christian life is defined solely by activity in behalf of the poor. Such activity is undoubtedly an indispensable aspect of Christian life, but it must be complemented by another. It is a fact that our neighbors, and especially the poor, are mediators of the encounter with Christ ("you gave it to me"), but according to the gospel, it is no less true that the "passage" through our relationship with Christ enables us to reach our neighbors themselves in a fuller way. Christ is the mediator between us and God the Father, but he is also mediator between human beings. Both commitment and contemplation are indispensable dimensions of Christian existence. I have had occasion to emphasize this point in various writings.

Your second question has to do with Marxist analysis. If I welcome the question, it is because it is one of those that most worry people and because the use of Marxist analysis has not always been correctly interpreted. I had an opportunity to deal with the subject in an article on "Theology and the Social Sciences," one of the writings that I submitted to this jury. I think the matter can be put briefly as follows.

The existence of boundless "inhuman poverty," to use the language of Medellín and Puebla, is a very important problem in liberation theology, because we want to engage in the best and most effective proclamation of the gospel possible in the circumstances. For this reason, we are concerned to know the situation of poverty and its causes (it is with the determination of these that problems begin). But since we are dealing with a social reality here, the situation and its causes must be analyzed by means of the social sciences.

Now, in the contemporary social sciences, and especially in the Latin American contribution to these sciences, concepts are used that come from Marxist analysis (but there are certainly also others from other sources). We have recourse to these in this area. At the same time, however, we do not attempt, or claim, to make an exclusive and complete use of Marxist analysis in liberation theology; much less do we attempt a kind of synthesis of faith and Marxist analysis. Furthermore, it seems to me for many reasons that such an attempt is meaningless. It goes without saying that the Marxist philosophy of the human person and of atheism has never played a part in liberation theology. On this point, my position is clear and emphatic.

An example here might be our use of the theory of dependence. This played an important part in the Latin American social sciences at the end of the 1960s. I made extensive use of the theory in *A Theology of Liberation*, but, as it happened, important Latin American Marxists regarded my use of it as non-Marxist. In the judgment of some of them, it was used in a perspective that even included points of view contrary to the Marxist thesis.

Let me pass to an especially burning issue: the question of class struggle. It is a question that elicits a whole range of emotions. That is why on other occasions I have referred to it as "social conflict." Let me clear up a first point: in my writings I have never regarded this conflict, or class struggle, as "the motive power of history" or as a "law of history." I have never used such vocabulary.

I dealt with this phenomenon at the level of social reality, as I made clear by citing a passage from a letter of Bishop Ancel in *A Theology of Liberation* (1988 ed., pp. 157–58). The pages I devoted to the subject there followed that document of the French episcopate in speaking of the class struggle as a fact. I think it important to add (as I did in my article "Theology and the Social Sciences") that the same acknowledgment of the fact is to be found in other documents of the magisterium. This recognition of the fact in no way signifies an endorsement of any rejection—not to say hatred—of persons as such. Such a rejection and hatred is unacceptable to a Christian and to any human being. I therefore reject any interpretation along this line of what I wrote on that occasion.

For me, the class struggle was a matter of pastoral concern, and that is how I dealt with it in *A Theology of Liberation*. For some Christians who were at that time beginning to involve themselves with the poor of Latin America, the social conflict of which they were having concrete experience raised questions difficult to answer. These had to do with the universality of Christian love and the unity of the church in a society with sharp internal divisions. The problem was how to live in fidelity to these aspects of the Christian message. Nor were there lacking some who thought that if the requirements were taken seriously and not reduced to vague abstractions, such fidelity was more or less impossible. I myself thought it important to reassert these aspects, but this could not be done without taking the bull by the horns.

In that same book, *A Theology of Liberation*, and in other writings, I speak of the social conflict not only between classes but also between races and cultures. But in order to tackle the problems in question, I thought it expedient to take the case that seemed the most difficult from the pastoral viewpoint, that of confrontation between social classes. The answer I developed in those pages (where I accepted the fact that the reality of class struggle, like all social conflict, exists at the level where it is subject to analysis by the social sciences, with all the nuances and evolution proper to these sciences) was that social conflict cannot be allowed to justify a denial of, or exception to, the universality of Christian love. This love is a fundamental requirement of the gospel message, for the love of God, to which we must bear witness, is given to every human being (to say otherwise is to distort the word of the Lord). This requirement was reasserted in a way that would decisively exclude any possibility of a Christian allowing hatred and the rejection of human beings as such to be an element in social confrontations.

In the same book I also maintained that the unity of the church is another fundamental datum of Christian teaching. This unity is a gift of the Lord and also something that human beings build up in the course of history.

It is clear, however, that these answers could not be pastorally effective unless people began by acknowledging the reality of situations that were causing problems for some. A further need was that they situate themselves, even if only as a working hypothesis, in the most difficult and conflictual situations. The theological formulations arrived at in these areas can always be improved—and I think I made some improvement in my later writings—but I believe, in all conscience, that the perspective of faith and pastoral concern was clearly present from the outset.

Bernard Sesboüé: With regard to the second subject I mentioned, I must say that you have already partially answered it when responding to the earlier questions in this discussion. In any case, I should like to formulate my question briefly.

You wrote as follows: "What is the relationship between salvation and the process of human liberation throughout history?" (*A Theology of Liberation*, 1988 ed., p. 83). In your answer you clearly set yourself against every form of dualism, and you were certainly right in doing so. As I read your works, I seemed to find that the relation between unity and distinction is the locus of a "symbolical overdetermination." Let me explain what I mean. Because human beings are bodily creatures, visible occurrences here on earth acquire the character of symbols and parables of the presence of salvation in our history. The utopia of the kingdom makes its way through human work. As a result, every step of progress in justice, moral sense, freedom, and well-being becomes a symbol of much more; it becomes an effective sign of salvation. The human liberations being brought about today benefit from the same "symbolical overdetermination." This is evident in the moral sense of the peoples who are aspiring to justice.

We must not forget, however, that faith functions as critic and as "negative theology" in relation to human liberations. It looks behind extreme situations and calls by its name the sin that distorts their objectives and methods. It transcends the movement of good as well as evil situations. It knows that those who are struggling for justice must themselves be converted. Does not this perspective of what I am calling "symbolical overdetermination" coincide, in its own way, with what you say based on the Ignatian expression, "contemplative in action"?

If I allow myself to put the question in these terms familiar to me as a Jesuit, I do so because it seems to me, as I read your most recent publications, that you are moving in this direction. Have I understood you correctly? Have you perhaps something more to say about this idea of unity in duality but without dualism?

Gustavo Gutiérrez: As you observed, I dealt earlier with this point in response to Christian Duquoc; I should like therefore to be brief here. I am in agreement with the perspective you point out and which you call "symbolical overdetermination." I do think that authentic human liberations are signs of, and advance payments on, a more comprehensive and deeper liberation: the liberation wrought by the redemptive grace of Christ. But the former are not identical with the latter. Since I have already said as much in *A Theology of Liberation*, let me cite a passage from it, although it uses language different than yours:

> Without liberating historical events, there would be no growth of the Kingdom. But the process of liberation will not have conquered the very roots of human oppression and exploitation without the coming of the Kingdom, which is above all a gift. Moreover, we can say that the historical, liberating event *is* the growth of the Kingdom

and *is* a salvific event; but it is not the coming of the Kingdom, not *all* of salvation [p. 177; 1988 ed., p. 104].

As regards the coincidence with "contemplative in action," I admit I have not made the connection. Nonetheless your suggestion seems to me a profitable one, and I feel that it helps me a great deal.

Bernard Sesboüé: One further question: Do you think your ideas have evolved between, on the one hand, *A Theology of Liberation* and *The Power of the Poor in History*, and, on the other, the presentation you made in defense of your "dissertation"?

Gustavo Gutiérrez: Yes, they have. My first book was written fifteen years ago and it remains what it was then. I, on the other hand, am alive and therefore absorbing new experiences and readings, carefully reflecting on the recent documents of the magisterium, having to respond to varying interpretations of my texts, perfecting the formulations of what I want to say, and shifting the emphases in the questions discussed. I must say, nevertheless, that I still identify with the basic ideas, plainly and simply because they were and continue to be less my own than those of the Latin American church and its basic ecclesial communities, which, under the impulse given by Vatican II, are endeavoring to proclaim the gospel on our continent. If this identification were no longer there, I would not have dared to offer my first book as a basis for this doctorate. On the other hand, if I had to write it today, I would have some different formulations and themes—in connection, for example, with the concrete condition of the poor, theological method, social analysis, the situation of women, spirituality, the present tasks of the church, and human rights. But does not the same thing happen to any theologian? Such an evolution seems to me quite unoriginal.

Now that I have answered your questions, Father Sesboüé, please allow me to touch on one point you made in your introductory remarks. Your observation on the *status confessionis* was, I think, a very acute and fruitful one. I find this approach very illuminating for an understanding of what we are trying to do in liberation theology when we remind people today and in our situation that the preference for the poor and the advancement of justice are fundamental in biblical revelation and the teaching of the church. To say this is, I think, to say what Christian Duquoc meant when he referred to the structural focus on the poor in liberation theology. We are dealing here with something that is located at the level of faith and not simply in the social and economic areas. This seems to me to be the central point in what we have tried to contribute to the life and thinking of the church.

I am very grateful for the traditional and yet personal way in which you formulate your point, and I believe it will greatly help us in our work. I think it in place to mention here how much this perspective of faith regarding the poor owes historically to that holy man, John XXIII, as well as to the testimony of Cardinal Lercaro—two men who were not Latin Americans!

Bernard Sesboüé: I am very satisfied with your answers.

Gustavo Gutiérrez: Thank you, Father Sesboüé.

Maurice Jourjon: Dear Gustavo, I ask your forgiveness, but because of the way this discussion of your dissertation is going, I am obliged to pick up the ball and pass quickly to the offensive.

I shall refer a good deal to your first book, because I think a person's first book always says something that cannot be misleading. I shall offer a judgment of your work that springs from a degree of incompetence but also from unreserved friendship. A degree of incompetence: because the theology I know best, that of the patristic period, is not likely to be of any great use in today's discussion; it must not be thought, however, that I am a stranger to or at odds with this discussion. An incompetence, on the other hand, only to a degree, for in my spirit and flesh and blood I have experienced a liberation in my own country and cannot but bow my head in the presence of Latin America's struggle for its liberation, even though I have no experience of it from the inside.

At the same time, my judgment is one inspired by unreserved friendship. It is a longstanding friendship that I allow myself to mention here because I knew you as a seminarian and student of theology and can attest to your sense of the church and the seriousness of your studies.

I should like to ask you about the problematic of your work. You write, for example: "The options which Christians in Latin

America are taking have brought a fundamental question to the fore: What is the *meaning of the faith* in a life committed to the struggle against injustice and alienation?" (*A Theology of Liberation*, 1988 ed., p. 74). Allow me first to recall the classic answer given by theology (although recalling it does not mean assenting to it); then I shall ask you why you think it necessary to depart from that classic position.

The classic answer is to say that faith has no direct meaning for a life of commitment to the struggle against injustice and alienation; the life of the theological virtues simply requires that this commitment be taken as seriously as any other duty of one's state, without concessions but also without excommunicating one's adversary in the name of the faith. I ask, then: Is it truly necessary—and if so, why—to go a step further, since, when all is said and done, this classic answer has enabled many men and women to commit themselves in a radical way to the struggle for justice?

Gustavo Gutiérrez: Why do I raise the question when the classic answer was good and correct? I would say that it is always useful to approach any question from the vantage point of other problems and in another vocabulary. This is evidently not the place for me to pass value judgments on my work. I do honestly believe, however, that I am traditional in the true sense of this term. I think that the ways in which this subject has been approached throughout the history of the church have much to say to us. In any case, I think that the question must be raised once more on the basis of the problems that have been raised and are being raised today in Latin America.

In my opinion—I say this in my book and am very clear on it in my own mind—the faith does not provide us with a social or political plan. Furthermore, it cannot provide such a plan. At the same time, however, I believe that poverty as we experience it in Latin America is not solely a social problem, and I think it worth taking up the question once more with that fact as a starting point. The depth and cruelty of a poverty that affects not merely isolated individuals but, unfortunately, a whole population, raises basic questions. That is why I think it good to return to the subject, for our problematic today is no longer quite the same as the classic problematic of faith and politics. I think the latter approach was inadequate for our experience today—not false but inadequate, in view of the fact that we were encountering, and still are, so inhuman a situation as that of the poverty in question.

This morning I tried to say something on this point. For myself, the entire situation raises questions of faith. And indeed my book is forever dealing with pastoral questions that persons formulated in some such words as these: "The majority of our people live in an inhuman situation that rejects the will of God. What has faith to say to me about this?" I would even say that the entire book is directed toward saying that the faith does have a meaning in response to the needs we experience in Latin America, in response to the unacceptable social injustice in which the poor are living.

That is why we reopen this classic subject: not, however, as simply a social or political question but as a comprehensive human question. This lends a certain novelty to the problem, although this does not keep us from looking for elements of an answer in earlier responses. The gospel is always the same, but we approach it in order that it may address our concerns. It is this that gives novelty to our historical journey, a novelty, however, that comes not from this or that theology but from the presence of the Spirit in the church.

Maurice Jourjon: You just said that your theology is traditional, and I think that in the best sense of the word this is profoundly true. That is why, when I read what you have to say about private and communal prayer or when I listened to your doctoral lecture this morning on theology and spirituality, I feel an inclination to ask you whether you would admit that your theology is, after all, of a monastic kind. By that I mean that it provokes a commitment and that this commitment sometimes calls for new forms of personal and communal life.

Gustavo Gutiérrez: In my view—and this is a partial affirmative answer to your question—there can be no Christian life without a contemplative dimension. But for that very reason I do not regard the contemplative life as the private property of monks but rather as a requirement laid upon every Christian, and not upon those alone who have chosen the monastic life.

With this in mind I would not be upset to have my theology

called a monastic theology, precisely because of its influence on the commitment you mentioned. A few minutes ago, Father Sesboüé briefly noted that I often cite St. Ignatius of Loyola. Indeed, I am not afraid to acknowledge that as far as spirituality is concerned, I am something of an Ignatian. I see myself as having been deeply impressed by the experience of St. Ignatius, which a first-generation disciple summed up in the phrase "contemplative in action." This makes a very fruitful point of departure. I cannot say, however, that the phrase represents the monastic focus, because it strongly emphasizes pastoral (or, in the case of the laity, political) action. I regard the Ignatian synthesis as very interesting and rich, but also very difficult.

Maurice Jourjon: My second question follows the line you took in your first answer. If your theology implies a way of looking at things, a practice, it will very rapidly — more rapidly perhaps than a monastic theology — run into the question of the practice of the sacraments. Given the deep and unjust social divisions that occur even among Christians, what is the significance for the eucharistic celebration?

Gustavo Gutiérrez: I welcome the question, which deals with a difficult, sometimes poorly understood, yet important matter. I belong to a people who have a strong sense of the sacraments, and with that people I live the faith and practice it. But the question you ask is also a tricky one. Either one takes the eucharist lightly and then one sees no difficulties. Or else one receives the eucharist as truly an anticipation of and call for a communion that we do not yet possess within history. In this case, how is it possible when celebrating the eucharist, when celebrating the death and resurrection of the Lord, not to have in mind all the things that shatter human fellowship, such as the injustices we see at the social level?

We already find this problematic in the letters of St. Paul and in writings of the fathers of the church. The problem arises if one takes the eucharist seriously. Poverty, radical social inequality, and the serious responsibilities that those in Latin America who call themselves Christians have in this situation — all these make the celebration of the eucharist a challenge for us. We must have the courage to see the difficulty; not to see it is to remain unaware of the real world and to be lacking in the respect due to the eucharist.

In my view, however, this is not a reason for not celebrating the eucharist; on the contrary, we must learn to become aware of the context that gives rise to the difficulties, while realizing also that we engage in this celebration as a journeying and sinful community. A Latin American said on one occasion that it is not possible to celebrate the eucharist at present because we are living in a situation of social injustice and that only when this situation is resolved will we have the conditions needed for an authentic celebration of the eucharist. I am in complete disagreement with this position, and I deal with it in *A Theology of Liberation.*

That position reminds me of the untenable thesis of a book I read during my first years in Europe; I am referring to Montuclard's *Les evénéments et la foi,* in which the author maintained we must first create a just society as a condition for being able to proclaim the gospel. As I see it, we do indeed celebrate the eucharist in a history branded by sin, but we celebrate it in the hope of a true communion both within history and beyond it. The eucharist is the celebration not of a finished human reality but of something being built; it brings a call to conversion, and indeed that is how we begin each eucharist. For this reason, the proper celebration of the eucharist with joy and thanksgiving for the Lord's gift must have consequences for the presence of Christians in history where they are to create a just and human world.

Jean Delorme: It is traditional at defenses of dissertations for us exegetes to find a mistake in the biblical citations of the doctoral work. I have reviewed your citations, and I must admit that they are all correct. Happily, your book, *We Drink from Our Own Wells,* allows me to save the honor of the exegetes. You cite Isaiah 61:1–2, but why did you not add v. 3, which is also connected with your subject? Something for a future reprint!

Let us turn to the questions. We scripture scholars always have difficulties with the use made of the Bible in theology. Why do you rely on von Rad in the matter of the creation-salvation relationship? Do you not think that the lack of a more thorough study of the Psalms is a defect in your work? What biblical hermeneutic do you follow? What do you mean when you say in *We Drink from Our Own Wells* that "the Bible reads us"?

Gustavo Gutiérrez: I shall begin with the question of hermeneutics. In my writings I try to do theology with a strong biblical basis, but not a work of exegesis in the strict sense. I believe that we approach scripture (which I for my own part receive in the church) in the context of our present situation; it is with the questions in mind that come to us from this situation that we read the scriptures. But the word of the Lord is not a repertory of answers to our questions; it addresses us and often changes our questions or raises others. That is what I wanted to say when I claimed that "it reads us." The phrase is a symbolic way of saying that between us and the scriptures there is not a one-way street but a circular relationship.

I think that a readiness to accept the judgment of scripture on us plays an important part in our reading of it. I say as much from the opening pages of *A Theology of Liberation.* We ought not to have recourse to the Bible in order to justify choices already made; in the long run this leads to manipulation of the Bible. I have always tried to avoid this course, even in its subtlest forms. Have I succeeded? Others can judge of this, and I will regard their views as quite important. In any case, I have always thought it very important to be attentive to the role of challenger that scripture plays when read in the church.

From my experience of reading the Bible with groups of the faithful I have learned the need of seeing the text as at once close and distant. When reading a particular passage in a Christian community, I have often heard someone saying by way of commentary: "That is exactly what happened to me yesterday." In the popular media we see a great closeness of the word. This feeling that the word of God is near is doubtless a fine thing, but it does not therefore cease to have its dangers. It is also necessary to see that the text is distant, having been written in another age and another culture; this means that in approaching the text one must take this otherness into account and one must have information about the Bible that is required for putting texts in their context.

This last point has a place in any pastoral experiment. But I think it has consequences at a more technical and theological level. It must be kept in mind that the scriptures speak to us today, but for them to do so it is required that we place them in their context and penetrate their meaning with all the help that the life of the church supplies down the centuries. All this will only bring out more fully the challenging aspect of the Bible that I mentioned a moment ago.

You touched on two other points. It is a fact that when I wrote *A Theology of Liberation* fifteen years ago, von Rad was a very important author for me. I think, moreover, that he was, and continues to be, one of the great names in Old Testament studies; my treatment of the relationship between creation and salvation owes much to his contribution; this accounts for the citations from his works. Time has passed since then; other reading as well as critical examinations of von Rad's great work have caused me to distance myself from one or another point of his thesis. But his work continues to be a classic in the field.

You are correct when you say that my writings contain no full and thorough discussion of the Psalms. I make many references to them, but that, of course, is not the same thing.

Jean Delorme: I should like to ask you to explain what you mean by a "militant reading" of the Bible. I have not found the expression in your more recent writings.

Gustavo Gutiérrez: No, you will not find it there or, for that matter, prior to the one article in which I took up the point. The phrase was a way of emphasizing something I regard as important—namely, the part that our Christian militancy plays in our reading of the Bible. As I said a moment ago, all of us approach the scriptures in the light of our own situation and experience. If persons make a commitment in a perspective springing from faith, this too leaves its mark on their approach; their commitment conditions them as readers, for they want now to see their Christian solidarity and activity in the light of the word. Their reading is made in the context of a committed, active, militant Christian life.

Jean Delorme: And the expression "social appropriation"?

Gustavo Gutiérrez: The expression "social appropriation" was intended to highlight the role of the communal perspective in making the scriptures our own, as opposed to a frequently individualistic reading. Individualism led to a "spiritualism," such as shows up in, for example, some readings of that beautiful text, the Magnificat. Such a reading strips the text of all its historical and eschatological incisiveness. "Appropriation" was also meant to remind us of the fact that members of the basic ecclesial communities increasingly feel the scriptures read in church to be theirs: not foreign to their lives but their very own.

Jean Delorme: When you speak of a reading in the context of committed, militant Christian life, I am in agreement. But it must not be forgotten that such a life already bears the mark of the word. The word precedes the commitment; at the beginning we have a spiritual experience. On the other hand, the text always eludes us; it is what you called "distant."

You discuss this spiritual experience as the point of departure for your book, *We Drink from Our Own Wells* (p. 37). I have a question with regard to it. Do you not think that in your commentary on John 1:35–42 (pp. 39–42) you pass very quickly from the fact that the group of disciples follow Jesus, to the claim that this following is a "collective adventure"? Would you explain more fully the scope you give to the word "collective"?

Gustavo Gutiérrez: I would say, to begin with, that in the book "collective" is used as a synonym of "communal"; there are passages that make this quite clear. My concern was to bring out the point that the following of Jesus always supposes membership in the assembly, the *ecclesia*. The following is, of course, a personal, free decision on my part, but I cannot live it out except in a community.

In the book the expressions "collective adventure" and "community enterprise" are used synonymously. They capture, I think, both the social and the personal element. When, in the final verses of Matthew's Gospel, the Lord describes the task to be done, he says it is to "make disciples of all nations." He obviously means "of all individuals," but without disregarding the fact that these individuals belong to human groups, to collectivities. We follow Jesus and become his disciples in a community, an assembly.

I do not think, therefore, that the passage from the call of the first disciples to the idea of the communal and collective is an overly rapid one; it is a passage that is already contained in the dynamism of faith, which is a gift of the Lord but also something freely and personally accepted. We live our faith in a community; this not only does not diminish the personal element but even gives it its full meaning.

Henri Bourgeois: I want to be brief, since we have been talking now for several hours. I shall begin by mentioning again the word "respect," which Father Sesboüé used earlier. I wish to greet with respect not only Gustavo Gutiérrez but all the Latin American friends who are in attendance, because of the witness he gives and because of his theological work. I wish also to call to mind Hugo Echegaray, a young Latin American theologian who studied and taught in our faculty and who died prematurely. Then, since so much has been said here of liberation, I would like to recall the laborious and even dangerous work being done by some theologians on other continents: in South Africa, in Poland, in countries of the East, and in some countries of Asia. They are all a source of great riches for the church.

I have some questions. The first: Can you tell us briefly what tasks you think lie ahead for the theology of liberation?

Gustavo Gutiérrez: I am very grateful to you for recalling Hugo Echegaray. In my opinion, his death was a great loss for the church in Peru and for Latin American theology. But his life and witness were a gift for which we shall always thank the Lord.

I shall be brief, despite the fact that the question could take us far afield. In liberation theology we are trying to talk of God in the context of the suffering of the innocent in Latin America. As a result, we deal with tricky matters in which it is difficult to express ourselves in a fully correct way. I think we must continually refine and perfect our language. It seems to me, too, that we must go more deeply into a basic and permanently valid insight: the connection between theological methodology and spirituality. This is something typical of us and closely connected with a fundamental position: that the ultimate reason for the preferential option for the poor resides in God, the Father whom Jesus Christ reveals to us.

There are still other themes already present in liberation theology that still need to be treated more fully: the racist element at work in the condition of the poor; the situation of women, especially those who are poor and are thus doubly oppressed and marginalized. These situations are expressions of the death that poverty brings with it, and the theology of liberation has been born precisely of the necessity of proclaiming the kingdom of life in a world marked by death.

Henri Bourgeois: I have been struck by your emphasis on gratuitousness both in your writings and today in this defense. What does analysis of human and natural realities and of second causes contribute to theological work?

Gustavo Gutiérrez: I myself am struck by gratuitousness — as a fundamental datum of our Christian life in relation to God, but also as a human quality. As I see it, without gratuitousness there is no authentic encounter among human beings. In every experience of love there is a need of gratuitousness, for no one is content to be loved for his or her attributes or merits. All look for something that goes deeper.

The encounter with God is also an encounter with ourselves. Those who believe in a God made human cannot separate the two aspects. This is why talk of gratuitousness is not a flight from the human world and from tasks within history. On the contrary. In his letter to Philemon Paul says: "I write to you, knowing that you will do even more than I say." Gratuitousness goes beyond the behavior required by justice. There is nothing more demanding, nothing more productive of commitment in daily life, than the gratuitousness that has its source in the love of God. To love others in a free and unmerited way is to love not only what they are but what they are capable of being; it is to have confidence in them. I think the attitude of gratuitousness gives the requirements of justice their full meaning.

Henri Bourgeois: What, in your opinion, does liberation theology have to say to European theology?

Gustavo Gutiérrez: We have, and quite legitimately, different addressees, different partners in dialogue. I do not think an attempt should be made to apply liberation theology mechanically to Europe. In Latin America we have suffered a great deal from interpretations imposed from outside our real situation, and we do not want to do the same thing ourselves in the opposite geographical direction.

We have different addressees, but European theology does not on that account cease to challenge us and raise questions for us. Something similar ought to be true of our theology in

Europe. A main point here in Europe would perhaps be to realize that among us poverty is not simply a social or economic matter. It is certainly that, but it is also something more. We are dealing with an all-embracing human situation, a real world one must enter if one is to understand the destructive power of poverty and feel the forces of death at work in it. But it is a world in which not everything is negative; rather, amid all the negative, there is a way of being persons. Amid this poverty that means death there is an experience of encounter with the Lord through solidarity with those who suffer.

Liberation theology is not simply, as some people here think, a theology that emphasizes the social dimension. It is that, but it is more; we are trying to take our stand at a point where it is impossible to separate solidarity with the poor from spirituality, brotherly and sisterly love from prayer, human beings from God. That is what it means to be a Christian, a disciple of Christ who is both God and man.

I think that a good number of European theologians have a growing understanding of our perspective. This is leading to approaches that will be very fruitful.

NOTE

1. In this "presentation" I have taken into account the remarks to be found in two documents: the Instruction *Libertatis nuntius*, on certain aspects of the theology of liberation, issued by the Congregation for the Doctrine of the Faith in September 1984, and the *Documento sobre la Teología de la Liberacíon*, published by the Peruvian episcopate in October 1984. The *Documento* says: "We urge those especially who are working at liberation theology to evaluate their studies and publications in the light both of the Instruction and of the present document" (no. 75). In this spirit I have tried to clarify, in this summary presentation (and in the theological discussion of my work that follows it), the train of thought developed in my writings; I hope thereby to forestall inadequate interpretations of it. The effort at clarification has given me an opportunity to reaffirm my communion with the magisterium and my will and desire to place my theological thinking at the service of the church's work of evangelization.

Chapter Two

Theology and the
Social Sciences
(1984)*

INTRODUCTION

Reflection on the word of God is intertwined with the way in which this word is lived and proclaimed in the Christian community. When a theology boldly, and in depth, makes its own the situation that the church is experiencing at a given moment of its history, then the context (including the past) in which the theology is born becomes important. The substantial permanence of such a theology is the result of its ability to sink its roots both in the real problems of its age and in the faith experience of a particular community of the followers of Jesus. This is undoubtedly the reason why the thought of an Augustine of Hippo and a Thomas Aquinas (to mention but two great names) challenges us even today.

In recent centuries, the theology developed at the great clas-

---

*This essay only attempts to present some reflections concerning the relation between these two disciplines in the Latin American context. It is beyond my purpose to offer a global treatment of Marxist thought in all its different aspects.

sic centers of thought was forced to deal with a state of affairs produced by what we know as the "modern mentality." This mentality reached its mature form in a lengthy process and received a decisive stimulus from the industrial and social revolutions of the eighteenth century, as well as from the intellectual consciousness expressed in the events we know as the Enlightenment.

At that time, the church found itself living in a social setting in which the faith and the Christian way of life were being subjected to demanding criticism. That period has not yet come to a close. Time has smoothed down some rough edges and polished others, but theologians are still dealing with the situation in an effort to give new vigor to the proclamation of the Lord's word in the modern world.

At the same time, however, a new situation, one brought about by the very nature of the modern age, has begun to surface. I am referring to the increasingly more forceful and widespread historical presence of the poor and oppressed of this world. In many instances, this presence has manifested itself suddenly and in unforeseen ways; the result has been a new set of conditions in which the Christian community must live. For this reason, there is talk of a real "irruption of the poor" into contemporary society and the contemporary church. But if we try to get inside the process, it becomes easy to see that the suddenness is more apparent than real. For the movement has, in fact, deep historical roots that ensure the permanence of the historical phenomenon and show that we are not dealing with a passing curiosity.

The theological projects that have been undertaken in the setting of the so-called Third World countries, among the racial and cultural minorities of the affluent countries, and in feminist circles, are expressions of the new presence of those who have hitherto been "absent" from history. These new projects have thus far been emerging in areas that have, theologically speaking, been barren but in which the Christian faith has ancient and deep roots. This fact explains the present fruitfulness of these areas.

One expression, among others, of these theological experiments is the discourse on the faith that has developed in the

Latin American setting and is known as liberation theology. The faith of the poor of that continent plays an important part in liberation theology, which is therefore concerned, as Medellín and Puebla were, to understand the situation of poverty, its causes, and the efforts of those suffering under it to escape from it. It is at this stage that recourse to the social sciences plays a significant part, for these sciences allow us to gain a more accurate knowledge of society as it really is and so to articulate with greater precision the challenges it poses for the proclamation of the gospel and thus for theological reflection as well. In the pages that follow, I shall limit myself to discussing the relationship between theology and the social sciences or, more accurately, to some aspects of this relationship.

A LANGUAGE FOR SPEAKING ABOUT GOD

Every theology is a discourse about God; in the final analysis, God is really the only theme of a theology. But the God of Jesus Christ comes to us as a mystery! A sound theology is therefore conscious that it is attempting something extremely difficult, if not impossible: to think and speak about this mystery. This accounts for the well-known warning of Thomas Aquinas: "We know more of what God is not than of what God is." It is important to be clear on this point at the very beginning of any discourse on the faith, for God is truly more an object of hope (which respects mystery) than of knowledge.

CONTEMPLATION AND COMMITMENT

How, then, are we to find a way of speaking about God? From the viewpoint of liberation theology it must be said that we must first contemplate God and put God's plan for history into practice and only then think about God. What this statement means is simply that adoration of God and the doing of God's will are necessary conditions for thinking about God. Only within the framework provided by mysticism and practice is it possible to develop a discourse about God that is both authentic and respectful of its object. It is in practice and, concretely, in our actions toward our neighbor, especially the poor, that we encounter the Lord, although at the same time this encounter deepens our solidarity with the poor and makes it more authentic. Contemplation and historical commitment are indispensable and interrelated dimensions of Christian existence. The mystery that is God reveals itself in contemplation and in solidarity with the poor. Contemplation and commitment make up what liberation theology calls practice, the "first act," which is Christian life itself; only then can this life inspire "second act," a process of reasoning.

Contemplation and practice constitute what may be called the phase of silence before God; theological discourse, for its part, is a speaking about God. Silence is the condition required for a loving encounter (in prayer and commitment) with God. Experience of the inadequacy of words to express the depths of the encounter will only make our language both richer and more unpretentious. Theology is discourse enriched by silence.

Reflection on the mystery of God is possible only in the context of the following of Jesus. Only when one walks according to the spirit can one think and proclaim the gratuitous love of God for every human being. Perhaps it is this connection between Christian life and theological method that is turning the base ecclesial communities of Latin America into agents of the theological presently being developed there.

All Christian life begins with a conversion, which means breaking with personal and social sin, and embarking on a new course. Conversion is a necessary condition for acceptance of the reign of God (see Mk. 1:14). It means abandoning our own way (see Lk. 10:21) and entering upon the way of others — namely, our neighbors and, in particular, the poor.

MYSTICAL LANGUAGE AND PROPHETIC LANGUAGE

From the viewpoint of theological reflection, the challenge posed by Latin America is to find a language about God that will spring from the situation and the suffering created by the unjust poverty in which the vast majority live (despised races, exploited social classes, marginalized cultures, discrimination against women). At the same time, however, it must be a discourse that inspires a people struggling for its own liberation. It is here, in this setting of sufferings and joys, uncertainties and certainties, generous self-surrenders and ambiguities, that our understanding of the faith must be continually formed.

I think it may be said that both a prophetic and a mystical language about God are coming to light in these lands marked by exploitation and hope, affliction and joy. The language of contemplation acknowledges that everything comes from the Father's free and unmerited love. The language of prophecy denounces the situation (and its structural causes) of injustice and despoliation in which the poor of Latin America are living. Thus Puebla speaks of learning to see "the suffering features of Christ the Lord" in "very concrete faces in real life" (no. 31; the "faces" are described in nos. 32-39).

When not accompanied by prophecy, the language of contemplation runs the risk of having no impact on the history in which God is at work and in which we find God. On the other hand, without the mystical dimension, prophetic language can narrow its vision and weaken the perception of God who makes all things new. "Sing to the Lord; praise the Lord! For he delivered the life of the needy from the hand of evildoers" (Jr. 20:13). Singing and setting free; thanksgiving and meeting the requirements of justice: such is the challenge set for any Christian who desires to move beyond possible spiritualistic evasions and political reductionisms, and be faithful to the God of Jesus Christ.[1]

The aim of these two languages is to transmit the gift of the kingdom of God as revealed in the life, death, and resurrection of Jesus. This is the heart of the message that we are discovering anew in the light of our own real world and that calls us together to form a community, an *ecclesia*, wherein we may attempt to think our faith. Theology is an ecclesial function. It is done within a church that has the task of bearing witness in history to the definitive life that overcomes death. Witness to the resurrection finds expression in the option for life in all its manifestations, since nothing lies outside the universal scope of God's reign. This witness to life (material and spiritual, personal and social, present and future) is especially important in a continent that bears the stamp of premature and unjust death, although it is also characterized by efforts to achieve deliverance from this oppression. The existence of such death and sin is a denial of the resurrection. The witness to the resurrection will therefore always be able to ask, mockingly: "Death, where is your victory?"

RELATION TO THE SOCIAL SCIENCES

Talk of the poverty now existing in Latin America inevitably calls for descriptions and interpretations of the massive reality. This concern was present from the first theological essays we prepared. The episcopal conferences of Medellín and Puebla also undertook such descriptions and interpretations, as have many other magisterial documents over the years. In both cases (allowance being made for the nuances proper to magisterial texts and theological works) the goal—which ought to be made clear at the outset—is to study social reality for purposes of a better understanding, in the light given by faith, of the challenges and possibilities that this reality presents to the church in its work of evangelization. In other words, recourse is had to social analysis in order to understand a situation—not in order to use this analysis in the study of matters more strictly theological.

SOCIAL ANALYSIS AND CRITICAL RESPONSE

As I have pointed out a number of times in my books, scientific application of the social sciences is undeniably in its early stages and still marked by uncertainties. Nonetheless, these sciences do help us understand better the social realities of our present situation. We need discernment, then, in dealing with the social sciences, not only because of their inchoative character, which I just mentioned, but also because to say that these disciplines are scientific does not mean that their findings are apodictic and beyond discussion. In fact, the contrary is true. What is really "scientific" does not seek to evade critical examination but rather submits to it. Science advances by means of hypotheses that give various explanations of one and the same reality. Consequently, to say that something is scientific is to say that it is subject to ongoing discussion and criticism. This state-

ment holds in a special way for the ever-new and changing field
of social realities.

The attitude of critical discernment has been continually
operative in my writings.[2] I explained it clearly at an important
meeting held over ten years ago by CELAM:

> Dependency is an obvious fact. ... A theory has been
> developed to explain it, but the theory is tentative and self-
> critical. ... Liberation theology takes the fact of depend-
> ency into account and cannot possibly avoid also taking
> the theory of dependency into account. It does so in a
> critical way. At the same time, however, it needs to be said
> that liberation theology must be more attentive to the var-
> iations in the theory of dependency and to the criticisms
> leveled against it; it must avoid generalizations and profit
> by other kinds of analysis and other levels [*Diálogos*, pp.
> 228-29].

The same critical approach (which expresses an authentic
rationality and personal freedom) must be taken to movements
of liberation. Like every human process, these are ambivalent.[3]
We must therefore be clear in our minds regarding them, not
out of any aversion to history but, on the contrary, out of loyalty
to the values they embody and solidarity with the individuals
committed to them.[4]

The longing for liberation is undoubtedly one of the "signs
of the times" in our age. "For many persons in various ways this
aspiration—in Vietnam or Brazil, New York or Prague—has
become a norm for their behavior and a sufficient reason to lead
lives of dedication" (*Liberation*, p. 21). In all these places, men
and women will have to be faithful to a quest for freedom that
no political system guarantees. This, even though the quest may
cost them their lives—in capitalist societies, but also in the world
of what today is called "real socialism." It was for this reason
that I rejected, thirteen years ago, the attitude of "those who
sought refuge in easy solutions or in the excommunication of
those who did not accept their pat answers, schematizations,
and uncritical attitudes toward the historical expressions of
socialism" (*Liberation*, p. 56).

Recent historical events have validated that rejection and have dispelled illusions regarding concrete historical systems that claim to eliminate all evils.[5] As a result, we have launched out upon new and more realistic quests; quests, too, that are more respectful of all dimensions of the human.

SOCIAL SCIENCES AND MARXISM

Elements of analysis which come from Marxism play a part in the contemporary social sciences that serve as a tool for studying social reality. This is true of the social sciences generally, even where they differ from or are opposed to Marx (as in the case, for example, of Max Weber). But the presence of these elements does not at all justify an identification of the social sciences with Marxist analysis, especially if one takes into account what Father Arrupe, in a well-known letter on the subject, called "the exclusive character" of Marxist analysis ("Letter on Marxist Analysis," December 1980, no. 6).

The Theory of Dependency

The very fact that liberation theology has regarded the theory of dependence as important for an analysis of the Latin American social situation is enough to prevent the kind of identification just mentioned. For this theory had its origin in a development of the social sciences proper to Latin America, and is held by prominent theoreticians who do not regard themselves as Marxists. Nor may we overlook the fact that representatives of Marxism have severely criticized the theory. We are dealing here with a very important point of theory. Marx said: "The industrially more developed countries only present the less developed with an image of their own future" (*Capital* I, 17). This outlook, however, the theory of dependency rejects. A Latin American social scientist writes that "to begin with, this theory challenged the supposedly 'linear' pattern of the evolution of human society and branded as 'eurocentric' Marx's observations on the subject."[6] Elsewhere, speaking of the views of Fernando Henrique Cardoso, the most important representative of the theory of dependency, the same writer says: Cardoso maintains a "theoretical posture that is worlds removed from that of Marx."[7]

The nature of this article does not permit me to dwell on this point or to offer further evidence or go into the matter in greater depth. My intention in harking back to the theory of dependency—which was very much to the fore in early writings on liberation theology[8]—is simply to make the point that neither the social sciences generally nor the Latin American contribution to them can be reduced to the Marxist version. I am not denying the contributions Marxism has made to our understanding of economic and social matters; I do, however, want the necessary distinctions to be clearly grasped.

Furthermore, the use (a critical use, as we have seen) of the theory of dependency does not mean a permanent commitment to it. In the context of theological work, this theory is simply a means of better understanding social reality.

Ideological Aspects and Marxist Analysis

In the contemporary intellectual world, including the world of theology, references are often made to Marx and various Marxists, and their contributions in the field of social and economic analysis are often taken into account. But these facts do not, by themselves, mean an acceptance of Marxism, especially insofar as Marxism embodies an all-embracing view of life and thus excludes the Christian faith and its requirements. The matter is a complex one and would require a close study of texts, a presentation of divergent interpretations in this area, and the resultant distinctions and critical observations. Without getting into details I shall state my views of some questions.

Let me begin by clarifying a first point. There is no question at all of a possible acceptance of an atheistic ideology. Were we to accept this possibility, we would already be separated from the Christian faith and no longer dealing with a properly theological issue. Nor is there any question of agreement with a totalitarian version of history that denies the freedom of the human person. These two options—an atheistic ideology and a totalitarian vision—are to be discarded and rejected, not only by our faith but by any truly humanistic outlook and even by a sound social analysis.

The question of how closely connected the ideological aspects of Marxism are with Marxist social analysis is a question much discussed in the social sciences. The same is true even within Marxism itself: for some Marxists (in a line represented by Engels and Soviet Marxism, to give two examples) Marxism is an indivisible whole; for others (Gramsci, J. C. Mariátegui, and many more) Marxist analysis or the scientific aspects of Marxism are not inseparably linked to "metaphysical materialism."

I must make it clear, however, that in the context of my own theological writings, this question is a secondary one. In fact, given the situation in which Latin America was living, it seemed to me more urgently necessary to turn to more clearly theological questions (in this I differed from European writings on similar subjects). That is why I wrote, in a note in *Liberation*:

> We hope to present soon a study of certain questions concerning the ambiguities in the use of the term *materialism* and the various conceptions of Marxism as a total conception of life or a science of history. We hope therefore to situate the vision of human nature and atheistic ideology in Marxism [p. 201, note 41].

In the promised study (the promise has only partially been fulfilled in courses and conferences), my intention was to deal in greater detail with the ideological and philosophical aspects of Marxism, as well as with the connection between these aspects and the more scientific levels of analysis. But my concern was equally to show that the contributions of Marxist analysis needed to be critically situated within the framework of the social sciences. Otherwise, the importance of these contributions is likely to be exaggerated both by their defenders and by their opponents.

Others have made a similar study and drawn similar boundaries. I wish to take part in the effort, and I hope for the opportunity to go into the matter more fully. But I must call attention to the fact that in a Christian perspective, importance does not attach exclusively to the theoretical side of the question. There are also pastoral concerns that are urgently important for all and especially for the church's magisterium. The latter has therefore issued several recent pronouncements on the subject and taken account therein of the new problematic and the set of theoretical and practical questions it raises. Thus the encyclical *Pacem in Terris* of John XXIII made some fruitful distinctions. The letter *Octogesima Adveniens* of Paul VI touched on the subject in an open and authoritative way, pointing out the values and dangers of Marxism in this area (see esp. no. 34); it also pointed out the connections between analysis and ideology in Marxism and described the conditions required of a work that would go more deeply into the subject. The Puebla Conference returned to the question (see no. 92 and esp. nos. 543-45); it also drew attention to the way in which these problems arise in the Latin American context.

The letter of Father Arrupe to which I referred earlier drew its inspiration from these documents of the magisterium. In that letter we find distinctions, appraisals, warnings, and rejections with which I am in full agreement and which must be taken into account both in pastoral practice and in any theoretical discussion of the subject.

THEOLOGY AND SOCIAL ANALYSIS

My purpose in my theological writings was stated in the opening of *Liberation*: "This book is an attempt at reflection, based on the gospel and the experiences of men and women committed to the process of liberation in the exploited and oppressed land of Latin America" (p. xiii) — in the light, therefore, of the gospel, and in a world of poverty and hope.[9]

At no time, either explicitly or implicitly, have I suggested a dialogue with Marxism with a view to a possible "synthesis" or to accepting one aspect while leaving others aside. Such undertakings were indeed frequent during those years in Europe (see the movement created by the Salzburg conversations in the 1960s) and were beginning to be frequent in Latin American circles. Such was not my own intention, for my pastoral practice imposed pressing needs of a quite different kind.

As I have reminded the reader, once the situation of poverty and marginalization comes to play a part in theological reflection, an analysis of that situation from the sociological viewpoint becomes important, and thinkers are forced to look for help from the relevant disciplines. This means that if there is a meeting, it is between theology and the social sciences, and not between theology and Marxist analysis, except to the extent that elements of the latter are to be found in the contemporary social sciences, especially as these are practiced in the Latin American world.[10]

Use of the social disciplines for a better understanding of the social situation implies great respect for the so-called human sciences and their proper spheres, and for the legitimate autonomy of the political order. The description that these sciences give of a situation, their analysis of its causes, the trends and searches for solutions that they propose — all these are important to us in theology to the extent that they involve human problems and challenges to evangelization. It is not possible, however, to deduce political programs or actions from the gospel or from reflection on the gospel. It is not possible, nor should we attempt it; the political sphere is something entirely different.

I said as much, and with all desirable clarity, on the very first page of *Liberation*:

> My purpose is not to elaborate an ideology to justify postures already taken, or to undertake a feverish search for security in the face of the radical challenges that confront the faith, or to fashion a theology from which political action is "deduced." It is rather to let ourselves be judged by the word of the Lord, to think through our faith, to strengthen our love, and to give reason for our hope from within a commitment that seeks to become more radical, total, and efficacious. It is to reconsider the great themes of Christian life within this radically changed perspective and with regard to the new questions posed by this commitment. This is the goal of the so-called *theology of liberation* [p. xiii].

In this area an insistent demand is made, motivated by the desire to do something concrete and active, but it can also distort the perspective and limits of theological reflection. In the dialogues sponsored by CELAM in 1973, this point was discussed;

the result was clarifications that are worth recalling here. One of the participants asked from his discipline, sociology, what strategic lines were to be followed that would bring the theology of liberation to bear on the great social problems of Latin America. This gave me an opportunity to reply that there are three things that may be asked of theology: "Liberation theology must be required to supply a concrete language. But we must not ask of theology what it cannot and ought not give."

It is not the function of liberation theology "to offer strategic solutions or specifically political alternatives. . . . In my opinion, the 'theology of revolution' set out on that path, but it seems to me that it was not a theologically sound course to follow; in addition, it ended up 'baptizing' revolution—that is, it did not acknowledge the autonomy proper to the political sphere." It is, however, right "to ask theology to play a part in the proclamation of the word," for this is in keeping with the nature of reflection that "positions itself in the light of faith and not in the light of sociology (I understand the temptations of sociologists; theologians, however, operate in the light of the faith as lived in the Christian community)."

Theology may also be asked to help us avoid losing a comprehensive vision of a given historical process and reducing it instead to its political dimension:

> Theology must be aware that the problem is not solved solely by economic, social, and political structures. Theologians must, on the contrary, be aware of deeper changes that can take place in the human person, of the search for a different kind of human being, of liberation in the many dimensions of the human and not just in the economic and political dimension, although, of course, all these aspects are closely connected.

Most importantly:

> theology must be asked to show the presence of the human relationship to God and the rupturing of that relationship at the very core of the historical, political, and economic situation; this is something that no social analysis can ever

bring to light. A sociologist will never come to see that sin—the breaking of the relationship with God and therefore with others as well—is at the very heart of any unjust situation. If a theology does not tell us this when it takes a social situation into account, then, in my opinion, theology is not reading the situation in the light of faith. Faith will not provide strategies, but it will indeed tell us, as Medellín says, that sin is at the heart of every breaking of brotherhood and sisterhood among human beings; it will therefore call for a particular behavior and an option [all these passages are from *Diálogos*, pp. 229-30].

In my view, the requirements and tasks I have outlined here are fundamental for theology. They are part of its proper sphere; what is unacceptable is to turn theological reflection into a premise in the service of a specific political choice. This statement does not suggest a lack of interest in the serious questions raised by the struggle for social justice; it signifies only that we must be clear regarding the scope and limits of every contribution to so vast and complex a subject.[11]

The presence of the social sciences in theology at the point when it is important to have a deeper understanding of the concrete world of human beings does not imply an undue submission of theological reflection to something outside it. Theology must take into account the contribution of the social sciences, but in its work it must always appeal to its own sources. This point is fundamental, for whatever the context in which theological reflection takes place, "theology must now take a new route, and in order to do so it will have to appeal to its own fonts" (*Power*, p. 60).

Furthermore, the absolutely indispensable use of some form of rational discourse in theological work does not mean an uncritical acceptance of that form or an identification with it:

Theology is not to be identified with a method of analyzing society or with a form of philosophical reflection on the person. . . . It never makes use of a rational tool without in some way modifying it. This is in the very nature of theology, and the entire history of theology is there to prove it (*Diálogos*, pp. 88-89).[12]

CONFLICT IN HISTORY

This is a sensitive area, one in which it is difficult at times to see our way clearly; it stirs strong feelings. At the same time, however, it is a subject that cannot be avoided.

The Pastoral Problem

Some persons say they are shocked that this aspect of reality should even be considered. Let me begin by saying that to a great extent I understand their reaction. No one agrees with a situation in which human beings come into conflict. And in fact the situation is not "acceptable," either humanly or in a Christian perspective. Conflict is undoubtedly one of the most painful phenomena in human life. We should like things to be different, and we ought to look for ways of getting rid of these oppositions, but on the other hand—and this is the point I want to make— we cannot avoid facing up to the situation as it actually is, nor can we disregard the causes that produce it. Neither can we give up on something urgently necessary: to see the situation in the light of faith and of the demands of the kingdom.

In this area, the most important biblical—and traditional— theme is that of the relationship between peace and justice. Peace is a gift brought by God's reign, but authentic peace presupposes the establishment of justice. Therefore, drawing their inspiration from Paul VI, the bishops at Medellín could say in quite specific terms: " 'If development is the new name for peace' (Paul VI), Latin American underdevelopment, with its own characteristics in the different countries, is an unjust situation that promotes tensions that conspire against peace" (*Peace*, no. 1).

Christians may not give up on the promotion of peace, but the peace they are promoting must be built on authentic, permanent, and just foundations. "Peace is, above all, a work of justice" (Medellín, *Peace*, no. 14). It is not possible, of course, to conceal the fact that this places us at times in boundary situations, where theological reflection advances only by trial and error, and where the result is often inadequate. Despite this, it is impossible that we should give up on trying, within our limits, to bring a faith-illumined clarity to these extreme situations.

The history of theological reflection on war, that deadly scourge of humanity, is an example of what I mean. European theologians have long and direct experience in this area, which we in other parts of the world do not always understand in all its details. Even so, their theological thinking on the subject has never been entirely satisfactory, because of the sensitivity and slipperiness of the subject itself. Theological reflection on war is always tentative and in process. The divergent and in some ways opposed positions recently taken by the North American and European episcopates on nuclear weapons are examples of what I am saying.[13]

Living in Latin America and trying to get close to the "inhuman wretchedness" (Medellín, *Poverty*, no. 1), the boundless and "antievangelical ... poverty" (Puebla, no. 1159) of its people, means living in the midst of conflict that we do not want and in which as human beings we cannot possibly take pleasure. But neither can we deny it. To deny it would be to deny our own selves as human beings who are bound in solidarity to our fellows and as Christians who must live out both the universality of God's love and God's preference for the poor. For this reason, I wrote in *Liberation*:

> To become aware of the conflictual nature of the political sphere should not mean to become complacent. On the contrary, it should mean struggling—with courage and clarity, deceiving neither oneself nor others—for the establishment of peace and justice among all people [p. 31].

It is perhaps not easy for those who lack direct experience of these situations to understand all the demands they make. For myself, the question I have always asked and have repeated at every step has been this: How are we to meet all the requirements of love of God in a situation of conflict in which individuals end up opposed to one another? To put it more concretely:

a situation in which persons and social groups or nations, with various forms of power at their disposal, confront other persons, groups, and countries that have no power and no historical importance. Once again, I see the question as urgent because of my pastoral experience. Many Christians who were committed to the liberation process, and were fully aware of the conflictual aspects of the situation, were having problems with regard to the meaning of Christian love in such a situation. I therefore thought it absolutely necessary to discuss the problem, and to do so in the language of the time.

A conviction presided over my thinking in this area: there are no situations, however difficult, that amount to an exception or a parenthesis in the universal demands of Christian love. It is not enough, however, simply to assert this conviction; it is also necessary to apply it to concrete situations and seek adequate answers. This is what I tried to do in *Liberation*, pp. 272-79 (of the 1st edition), while allowing for all the difficulties and risks involved. There I focused on one manifestation—perhaps the most extreme and problematic, in the judgment of many Christians—of conflict within history—namely, the fact of class struggle. I thought it my pastoral duty not to shrink from this hard question, which many were asking at that time as they confronted various events and political situations in Latin America. In my discussion of the subject the conclusion I reached was clear: "it must be a real and effective combat, not hate. This is the challenge, as new as the gospel: to love our enemies" (*Liberation*, p. 276, 1st edition). That requirement comes from the universality of God's love.

A QUESTION OF FACT

My purpose at that time was to pose the pastoral and theological problem of love of neighbor in light of the historical fact of conflict, including the struggle between classes. Let me specify several points in this regard.

To speak of conflict as a social fact is not to assert it apodictically as something beyond discussion, but only to locate it at the level of social analysis. I cannot, for pastoral or theological reasons, simply deny social facts; that would be to mock those

Christians who must confront these facts every day. For this reason I made the following statement over ten years ago, during a discussion of the subject and at a bishop's request:

> The problem facing theology is not to determine whether or not social classes are in opposition. That is in principle a matter for the sciences, and theology must pay careful attention to them if it wishes to be au courant with the effort being made to understand the social dimensions of the human person. The question, therefore, that theology must answer is this: If there is a struggle (as one, but not the only form of historical conflict), how are we to respond to it as Christians? A theological question is always one that is prompted by the content of faith—that is, by love. The specifically Christian question is both theological and pastoral: How are Christians to live their faith, their hope, and their love amid a conflict that takes the form of class struggle? Suppose that analysis were to tell us one day: "The class struggle is not as important as you used to think." We as theologians would continue to say that love is the important thing, even amid conflict as described for us by social analysis. If I want to be faithful to the gospel, I cannot disregard reality, however harsh and conflictual it may be. And the reality of Latin America is indeed harsh and conflictual [*Diálogos*, pp. 89-90].

The conditional sentence ("Suppose that analysis . . . ") in that paragraph is important for situating the problem, for it leaves the door open, in an undogmatic way, to other possibilities.[14]

I spoke earlier in these pages of the critical stance to be maintained toward social analysis, but also of a proper acknowledgment of its contribution.

When I speak of conflict in history I always mention different aspects of it. That is why I continually refer to races discriminated against, despised cultures, exploited classes, and the condition of women, especially in those sectors of society where women are "doubly oppressed and marginalized" (Puebla, no. 1134, note). In this way, I take into account the noneconomic factors present in situations of conflict between social groups. The point of these constant references is to prevent any reduction of historical conflict to the fact of class struggle. I said earlier that in *Liberation*, pp. 272-79 (of the 1st edition) I was discussing the class struggle aspect of the general problem because it is the one that poses the most acute problems for the universality of Christian love. If it is possible to clear that obstacle, then we have an answer to the questions raised by other, perhaps less thorny, kinds of conflict. For it is evident that history is marked by other forms of conflict and, unfortunately, of confrontation between persons.[15]

There are those who seem without further discussion to identify the idea of class struggle with Marxism. As we know, this is incorrect and indeed was rejected by Marx himself. In his well-known letter to J. Weydemeyer (cited in *Liberation*, p. 284, note 51, of the 1st edition), he says: "As for me, mine is not the merit to have discovered either the existence of classes in modern society or the struggle between them. Much before me bourgeois historians had described the historical development of this class struggle and the bourgeois economists had studied its economic anatomy."

Marx thought that his own contribution was to have established the connection between class struggle and economic factors (as well as the dictatorship of the proletariat). These economic factors are often presented as operating historically in a deterministic manner. I am not concerned here with the important debate on this point or with the varying interpretations that the debate has produced within Marxism itself. The point I want to make is simply that an economically based determinist view of class struggle is completely alien to liberation theology.[16]

In this connection, experts on Marx have always pointed out the very limited space (a few paragraphs amid thousands of pages) given to class struggle in Marx's principal work, *Capital*. These various considerations have led to such statements as the following:

In Marx's view, the class struggle is not an essential part of his teaching, as others sometimes think. In the *Com-*

munist Manifesto he regards it indeed as necessary, given the fact of alienation, but it is a passing stage and by no means permanent. The truly essential focus of his humanism is the search for harmony among all through work, for an equality in that which is the distinctive element in human existence. But interpretations of Marxist thought as egalitarian are likewise shallow and without foundation. Marx recognizes the variations in gifts, qualifications, and so on. What he seeks is equality among classes in that which is specifically human: work deliberately and responsibly undertaken.[17]

Despite all this, Marxist thought does contain expressions that turn class struggle from a simple fact into "the driving force of history" and, in more philosophical versions, a "law of history." An analysis would have to be made to determine the meaning and importance of this transformation of fact into historical principle. My only concern here is to insist that this approach does not reflect my own thinking and that therefore I have never used such expressions.

THE MAGISTERIUM AND CLASS STRUGGLE

The acceptance of class struggle as a fact can be found in a number of magisterial documents. Here is a quick review.

The encyclical *Quadragesimo Anno* has some passages that are very clear on this point. These passages are always concerned with facts and certainly do not justify the situation. The pope says, for example: "In actual fact, human society now, for the reason that it is founded on classes with divergent aims and hence opposed to one another and therefore inclined to enmity and strike, continues to be in a violent condition and is unstable and uncertain" (no. 82). He immediately goes on to say: "As the situation now stands, hiring and offering for hire in the so-called labor market separate men into two divisions, as into battle lines, and the contest between these divisions turns the labor market itself almost into a battlefield where, face to face, the opposing lines struggle bitterly" (no. 83).

Further on, speaking of socialism and the ways in which it

differs from communism, the pope writes: "If the class struggle abstains from enmities and mutual hatred, it gradually changes into an honest discussion of differences founded on a desire for justice, and if this is not that blessed social peace that we all seek, it can and ought to be the point of departure from which to move forward to the mutual cooperation of the industries and professions" (no. 114). This passage does not simply refer to a social fact but claims that if the class struggle is approached in a certain way (in which all hatred is set aside), it can ultimately turn into "an honest discussion."

Two years after the council a group of bishops from various parts of the world wrote as follows:

> Governments must set about putting an end to this class struggle, which, contrary to what is commonly thought, has often removed all restraints from the rich, who continually achieve their ends at the expense of the workers and exploit them through insufficient wages and inhuman working conditions. For a long time now, the monied class has craftily conducted a subversive war throughout the world, slaughtering entire peoples in the process. It is time for poor peoples, supported and led by their legitimate governments, to defend their right to life in an effective way [Message of Third World Bishops, signed by eighteen bishops from various continents, August 1967].

In *Liberation* (pp. 157-58) I cited the following passage from a document the French episcopate issued in 1968:

> Oppression of the workers is a form of class struggle to the extent that it is carried on by those managing the economy. For the fact of class struggle must not be confused with the Marxist interpretation of this struggle. *The class struggle is a fact* that no one can deny. If we look for those responsible for the class struggle, the first are those who deliberately keep the working class in an unjust situation, oppose its collective advancement, and combat its efforts at self-liberation. Its actions do not indeed justify hatred of it or violence directed against it; it must nevertheless be

said that the "struggle for justice" (to use Pius XII's expression), which is what the struggle of the working class is, is in itself conformed to the will of God.[18]

Medellín, for its part, says that the opposition becomes more intense "in those countries that are characterized by a marked *biclassism*, where a few have much (culture, wealth, power, prestige) while the majority has very little" (*Peace*, no. 3; emphasis added). Following John Paul II, Puebla speaks of "structural conflict." Referring to present tendencies in Latin America that favor the appropriation of wealth "by a privileged minority" and, on the other hand, "are responsible for the poverty of a large majority of our people," the Puebla document says: "So there arises a grave structural conflict: 'The growing affluence of a few parallels the growing poverty of the masses' (John Paul II, Opening Address, III, 4)" (Puebla, nos. 1208-9).

Finally, John Paul II has discussed this point extensively and in depth in his encyclical *Laborem Exercens* on human work. In Section II, which bears the title, "Conflict between Labor and Capital in the Present Phase of History," he writes:

> Throughout this period, *which is by no means yet over*, the issue of work has of course been posed on the basis of the *great conflict* that in the age of and together with industrial development emerged between "capital" and "labor," that is to say, between the *small* but highly influential group of entrepreneurs, owners, or holders of the means of production, and the *broader multitude* of persons who lacked these means and who shared in the process of production solely by their labor [no. 11; emphases added].

This situation was due to exploitation of the workers by "entrepreneurs. . . . following the principle of maximum profit" (ibid.). A few pages further on, the pope repeats his point that behind a seemingly abstract opposition there stand concrete living human beings:

> It is obvious that when we speak of opposition between labor and capital, we are not dealing only with abstract

concepts or "impersonal forces" operating in economic production. Behind both concepts there are persons, *living, actual persons*: on the one side are those who do the work *without being the owners* of the means of production, and on the other side those who act as entrepreneurs and who *own* these means or represent the owners [no. 14, emphases added].

The people can therefore conclude: "thus the issue of ownership or property enters from the beginning into the whole of this difficult historical process" (ibid.).

We are, then, dealing with an opposition between real, living persons and not simply with a confrontation between abstract concepts or anonymous forces. The superiority of persons over things, which is one of the most important points made in the encyclical, applies here once again in a very painful area.

The passages are clear. The pope does not shrink from pointing out a harsh and painful situation. The truth is that only when we face these facts is it possible to pass a Christian judgment on them and give guidelines for rising above them. This is precisely what was already being done in the earlier documents I have cited.

THE REQUIREMENTS OF CHRISTIAN LOVE

Neutrality and Solidarity

I have been criticized for saying that when faced with a situation of this magnitude, neutrality is impossible and that it calls for our active participation. And yet the context of my statements made it clear that passivity or indifference is not permissible when the issue is justice and the defense of the weakest members of society. Passivity or indifference would be neither ethical nor Christian. This does not mean that the alternative is to promote conflict. "Those who speak of class struggle do not 'advocate' it—as some would say—in the sense of creating it out of nothing by an act of [bad] will. What they do is to recognize a fact and contribute to an awareness of that fact" (*Liberation*, p. 274, 1st edition). They acknowledge, that is, the reality of social conflict and the necessity of becoming aware of it so as to get rid of it by attacking its causes.

In this area John Paul II has made an enlightening distinction. In no. 11 of *Laborem Exercens* he says:

> This conflict, interpreted by some as a socio-economic class conflict, found expression in the ideological conflict between liberalism, understood as the ideology of capitalism, and Marxism, understood as the ideology of scientific socialism and communism, which professes to act as spokesman for the working class and the worldwide proletariat. Thus the real conflict between labor and capitalism was transformed into a systematic class struggle conducted not only by ideological means, but also and chiefly by political means.

The "real conflict" takes place in the factual world, and it is to this that the reflections in the same number of the encyclical apply. This real conflict can be transformed into a "systematic class struggle" as an all-embracing political strategy. The latter was not my position when I raised the question of the existence of conflict and the demands it makes of us. The real conflict and the systematic class conflict are two different things: that is precisely my own position. Confusions in this area are indeed possible, but for that very reason the pope's distinction between reality and strategy is especially enlightening.

The facts are hard to grasp and disputed, but this does not excuse us from a necessary option. The real issue here, the real requirement, is solidarity. I realize, of course, that if we evade the issue with a few general phrases or if we simply recall the principles regarding social conflict, we will have fewer problems. But it is not possible to remain neutral in face of the situation of poverty and the justice of the claims made by the poor. John Paul II has often reminded us of this truth, especially in the high expression of his teaching office that is the encyclical *Laborem Exercens*. Here he calls upon Christians and the entire church to commit themselves to movements of solidarity with workers (no. 8).

These movements arose, he says, as an ethical reaction

against "the degradation of humankind as the subject of work and against the unheard-of accompanying exploitation in the field of wages" (ibid.). For that reason, "following the lines laid down in the encyclical *Rerum Novarum* and many later documents of the church's magisterium, it must be frankly recognized that the reaction against the system of injustice and harm that cried to heaven for vengeance and that weighed heavily upon workers in that period of rapid industrialization was justified from the point of view of social morality" (ibid.).

All this is not simply past history. "There must be continued study of the subject of work and of the subject's living conditions. In order to achieve social justice in the various parts of the world, in the various countries and in the relationships between them, there is a need for ever new movements of solidarity of the workers and with workers" (ibid.). More than that, the pope says that "the church is firmly committed to this cause for she considers it her mission, her service, a proof of her fidelity to Christ, so that she can truly be the 'church of the poor' " (ibid.).[19]

No one is unaware of what this solidarity of the church with worker movements (a solidarity the pope looks upon as a "proof of her fidelity to Christ") means concretely. The church's task amid the social confrontations that this solidarity implies is to proclaim the gospel of love, peace, and justice. We know what consequences this solidarity has entailed for many Christians in Latin America, where confrontations are becoming more acute. The case of Archbishop Romero is a clear, painful, and yet happy example of this evangelical witness. But there are also the accusations brought against and the harassments suffered by so many other members (laity, religious, priests, and bishops) of the church in Latin America.

There is obviously no question of identifying a preferential option for the poor with an ideology or a specific political program that would serve as framework for reinterpreting the gospel or the task of the church. Nor is there any question of limiting oneself to one sector of the human race. I regard these reductive positions as utterly alien. But I have dealt with this matter on various occasions and need not insist on the point once again.

I do, however, wish to discuss a question I regard as important. I said earlier that the universality of Christian love is incompatible with any exclusion of persons but not with a preference for some. I think it worth citing here a passage from Karl Lehmann, a theologian and presently archbishop of Mainz:

> There can undoubtedly be situations in which the Christian message allows only one course of action. In these cases the church is under the obligation of decisively taking sides (see, for example, the experience of Nazi dictatorship in Germany). In these circumstances, an attitude of unconditional neutrality in political questions contradicts the command of the gospel and can have deadly consequences.[20]

There is no passage in my own writings that so incisively stresses specificity and points to one course of action as the only possible course. But, faced with so strong a statement, I cannot but ask: Does not what held for the experience of Nazism in Europe hold also for the Latin American experience of wretchedness and oppression? In both cases, we are faced with boundary situations, but that is precisely what I said at the beginning of this section, and it is to this kind of situation that Archbishop Lehmann is referring.

The important point is that according to the German theologian there are cases in which "the Christian message allows only one course of action." Would anyone dare brand this claim unchristian and reductivist? In this case, proximity to the horror of Nazism showed that the claim is theologically acceptable in an extreme situation. In such situations, the judgment one makes depends not simply on social analysis but on the ethical reaction (see John Paul II's notion), which we experience in face of a situation that we analyze and, above all, live through. Perhaps it is this very last point—living in the situation—that makes the difference in outlooks. For there is no doubt that behind Archbishop Lehmann's words lies the complex and painful experience of the German people and German Christians.[21] But there are other experiences no less painful and scandalous.

The Universality of Christian Love

All that has preceded brings me to a final, but fundamental, point. When we speak of taking social conflict (including the fact of class struggle) into account and of the need of overcoming the situation by getting at the causes that give rise to it, we are asserting a permanent demand of Christian love. We are thus recalling a basic injunction of the gospel: love of our enemies. In other words, a painful situation that may cause us to regard others as our adversaries does not dispense us from loving them; quite the contrary. When, therefore, I speak of social conflict, I am referring to social groups, classes, races, or cultures, and not an undue rejection of individuals.

There are indeed times in the struggle for justice when conflict may seem to be with individuals. Speaking of unions, John Paul II says:

> They are indeed a mouthpiece for the struggle for social justice, for the just rights of working persons in accordance with their individual professions. However, this struggle should be seen as a normal endeavor "for" the just good: in the present case, for the good that corresponds to the needs and merits of working persons associated by profession; but it is not a struggle "against" others [*Laborem Exercens*, no. 20].

He goes on to say, more specifically: "Even if in controversial questions the struggle takes on *a character of opposition* toward others, this is because it aims at the good of social justice, not for the sake of 'struggle' or in order to eliminate an opponent" (ibid., emphasis added). In these difficult questions there is indeed a de facto opposition between persons, but even amid this opposition the Christian ethos does not allow hatred.

In *Quadragesimo Anno* Pius XI acknowledged the existence of class struggle and even accepted it in some situations as something that can gradually change "into an honest discussion of differences founded on a desire for justice" and that "can and ought to be the point of departure *from which to move forward* to the mutual cooperation of industries and professions" (no. 114). But he also pointed out a basic condition required for that kind of change and progress: "if class struggle abstains from enmities and mutual hatred." This is indeed an absolutely fundamental Christian requirement.

The same call for a universal Christian love is to be found in the other passages I have cited regarding what John Paul II calls "the real conflict" between social classes. Bishop Lehmann also reminds us of the same obligation in words that continue the already cited passage regarding situations in which neutrality on the part of the church "contradicts the command of the gospel and can have deadly consequences." He goes on to say, and rightly: "But when seen from the viewpoint of the gospel, a decisive commitment to specific groups must never be allowed to overshadow a fundamental part of the Christian message — namely, that the church has an obligation to communicate God's love to all human beings without exception."[22] Even the extreme case, "in which the Christian message allows only one course of action," does not do away with the requirement of universal love. This is all the more true, then, when there is question of respecting both the universality of love and the preferential option of which I have spoken. This point has always been clearly made in my writings, and I have always regarded it as fundamental.

CONCLUSION

I am fully conscious of how vast and complex the problems are that I have discussed in these pages. They undoubtedly require further study, but I think that what I have written will help readers to recall my position and make clear the problems I have dealt with.

The work of theology starts with faith in the revealed word, which we receive and live out in the church. It is work done in the light of faith and has for its ultimate purpose a greater fidelity to the Lord and the proclamation of the gospel.

To be a Christian is to be a witness to the resurrection and to proclaim the reign of life. We celebrate this life in the eucharist, which is the primary task of the ecclesial community. In the breaking of the bread we remember the love and fidelity that brought Jesus to his death; we remember, too, his resurrection, which was the confirmation of his mission, a mission to all and especially to the poor. At the same time, the breaking of bread is both point of departure and point of arrival for the Christian community. In it the assembled faithful express their deep communion in human suffering (often caused by the lack of food) and joyfully acknowledge the risen Lord who gives life and raises the hope of the people he has brought together by his actions and his word.

The theology of liberation seeks to provide a language for talking about God. It is an attempt to make the word of life present in a world of oppression, injustice, and death.

—*First published in* Páginas, *nos. 63-64, September 1984*

NOTES

1. These themes are developed more fully in my book *El Dios de la vida* (Lima, 1982). The following short titles will be used in this article: *Liberation* = *A Theology of Liberation: History, Politics, and Salvation* (Maryknoll, N.Y.: Orbis Books, 1973; quotations will, unless otherwise indicated, be from the new edition of 1988); *Vida* = *El Dios de la vida*; *Power* = *The Power of the Poor in History* (Maryknoll, N.Y.: Orbis Books, 1983); *Drink* = *We Drink from Our Own Wells: The Spiritual Journey of a People* (Maryknoll, N.Y.: Orbis Books, 1984); *Diálogos* = *Liberación: Diálogos en el Celam* (Bogotá, 1974). The translation of the encyclical *Laborem Exercens* is from *Origins*, 11 (1981-82): 225-44.

2. Karl Lehmann criticizes the use of the theory of dependency but acknowledges that "some writers realized the theory requires certain corrections"; see his essay, "Problemas metodológicos y hermenéuticos de la 'teología de la liberación,'" in the report of the International Theological Commission, *Teología de la liberación* (Madrid: BAC, 1978), p. 34 and note 73. I do not neglect Lehmann's critical assessment of Latin American liberation theology. At the same time, however, I think it fair to say that, despite disagreements about it, this theology is a serious enterprise that calls for dialogue and reflection.

3. See *Drink*, pp. 2-3: "The situation is not a simple one, and we must not let ourselves be naive about it. The challenges come from various quarters. Our present situation is beset with difficulties and possibilities; equivocal solutions prompted by despair are offered, but so are lines of action that respect the deepest human values. Incredible self-centeredness and pride of every kind make their appearance, but so do acts of humble and unlimited generosity. Some enthusiasts want to make everything over, while others urge creative undertakings that

are marked by sensitivity to the most worthwhile traditions of the Latin American peoples."

4. See *Liberation*, p. 21: "We are not suggesting, of course, that we should endorse without question every aspect of this development of ideas. There are ambiguities, critical observations to be made, and points to be clarified."

5. See studies of the "real socialism" to which I referred above.

6. Agustín Cueva, "El uso del concepto de modo de producción en América Latina: algunos problemas teóricos" in *Modos de producción en América Latina* (Lima, 1976), p. 24.

7. Ibid., p. 26.

8. Medellín, too, appeals to this interpretation of the Latin American situation: "We refer here, particularly, to the implications for our countries of dependence on a center of economic power, around which they gravitate. For this reason, our nations frequently do not own their goods, or have a say in economic decisions affecting them. It is obvious that this will not fail to have political consequences given the interdependence of these two fields" (*Peace*, no. 8).

9. See *Liberation*, pp. 155-56: "The incertitude and apprenticeship involved in this task should not lead us to disregard the urgency and necessity of taking stands or to forget what is permanent—that the gospel annunciation opens human history to the future promised by God and reveals God's present work. On the one hand, this annunciation will indicate that in every achievement of fellowship and justice among humans there is a step toward total communion. By the same token, it will indicate the incomplete and provisional character of any and every human achievement. The gospel will fulfill this function based on a comprehensive vision of humankind and history, and not on partial focuses, which have their own proper and effective instruments of criticism."

10. See *Power*, p. 192: "This is why the popular movement is also the locus of encounter of the social sciences and Marxist analysis with theology—an encounter, to be sure, involving criticism of theology, and an encounter undertaken within the dynamics of a concrete, historical movement that transcends individuality, dogmatisms, and transitory enthusiasms. Hence any and all intellectual terrorist tactics simply miss the mark."

11. In another dialogue at this meeting, I said with regard to questions of a political kind: "It seems to me that we must avoid offering programs based on the faith, for then we would have an all-embracing integrism" (*Diálogos*, p. 259).

12. See *Power*, p. 56: "Theology always involves a reasoning process, though it is not necessarily identified with it."

13. See especially the important pastoral letter of the U.S. bishops on world peace, May 1983.

14. In the same section of *Diálogos* I said: "If some other kind of analysis should improve on the one I am now using, then, it seems to me, it will enrich my understanding of a situation that is one of wretchedness, injustice, and oppression" (p. 88).

15. The Peruvian bishops take the same approach: "Above all, it is necessary to acknowledge not only the existence of social conflicts but also the social structure of many of them, for they spring from the fact of opposed interests. It may even be admitted that these conflicts will never be definitively resolved so long as the opposed interests exist. But the conflicts and oppositions are not of their nature irreconcilable. It is much less possible, however, to accept the deliberate exacerbation of the conflicts. In our view, the correct application of distributive justice and the establishment of institutions and structures that truly embody this justice can overcome the conflicts and antagonisms" (*Documento sobre la teología de la liberación*, October 1984, no. 39). Compare the interesting reflections of R. Antoncich, *Christians in the Face of Injustice: A Latin American Reading of Catholic Social Teaching* (Maryknoll, N.Y.: Orbis Books, 1987), pp. 127-43.

16. See *Liberation*, p. 56: "There is also present in this process of liberation, explicitly or implicitly, a further ramification which it is well to keep in mind. The liberation of our continent means more than overcoming economic, social, and political dependence."

17. A. López Trujillo, *La concepción del hombre en Marx* (Bogotá: Editorial Revista Colombiana, 1972), p. 178.

18. Note signed by Alfred Ancel, auxiliary bishop of Lyons, in *Documentation catholique*, vol. 65, no. 1528 (November 17, 1968): 1950 (emphases in the text).

19. For an analysis of this point in the encyclical, see G. Gutiérrez, "El Evangelio trabajo," in *Sobre el trabajo humano* (Lima: CEP, 1982).

20. Lehmann (n. 2), p. 37.

21. On several occasions, persons have expressed surprise at not finding an extended treatment of the theme of violence in any of my works. They have even come up with some odd assumptions by way of explanation. In fact, the reasons for the omission are simple. I shall give the two most important.

The first is that theological reflection on violence or in this case, to be more accurate, counterviolence, has not advanced substantially beyond Thomas Aquinas. That teaching has been recalled in our time by Paul VI in his encyclical *Populorum Progressio*, no. 31, a passage that in turn was Medellín's inspiration in its document on *Peace* in the context of Latin America. Subsequently, the bishops of Nicaragua issued a statement in June 1979. All these are recent and clearly worded documents that called for no further emphasis from me.

The second reason is that, unlike other theological approaches (the theology of revolution, for example), my concern was to try to situate what is happening in Latin America in the broad channel of total liberation. This process is one that, in the final analysis, must be viewed in the light of God's word. The latter supplies the context in which to deal with subjects such as counterviolence that otherwise end up either bulking abnormally large or being treated solely at the level of principles. Such a fate is tragic, to say the least, in the case of violence.

22. Lehmann (n. 3), p. 37.

Chapter Three

The Truth Shall
Make You Free
(1986)

INTRODUCTION

In recent years we have seen the appearance of numerous news items, reports, and books on the theology of liberation; they have overflowed the boundaries of the church and found a place in the general communications media. They owe their existence to a heated discussion of the subject and are therefore of unequal value. During this period it has not been easy for readers who lack a specialized background to take a position in this crossfire of alleged condemnations and fervent defenses, of simplifications and more substantial works.[1]

The recent publication of the second Instruction of the Congregation for the Doctrine of the Faith, "Christian Freedom and Liberation" (*Libertatis Conscientia*; henceforth *LC*), provides an opportunity for clarifying many points. This instruction was promised in, and complements, an earlier document of 1984 from the same Congregation: "Instruction on Certain Aspects of the Theology of Liberation" (*Libertatis Nuntius*; henceforth *LN*). The latter contained important critical observations and at the same time spoke of a further document that would deal with "the theme of Christian freedom and liberation in its own right" and would "detail in a positive fashion the great richness of this theme for the doctrine and life of the church" (*LN*, Introduction). The promise has been kept; if we add to the new instruction the message that John Paul II sent shortly afterward in a letter, under his own signature, to the Brazilian bishops at their annual conference (henceforth *Message*), we have before us the shape of a new stage in the discussion of liberation theology.[2]

The discussion is ongoing, and this is healthy; the debate must continue, as Cardinal Ratzinger said a short time ago in an interview,[3] because the questions raised are central to the Christian faith and to the church's mission today. In addition, the clarification effected in recent years, as well as the documents already mentioned, are making the essentials stand out more clearly, pinpointing with greater precision the problems to be resolved, and setting the tone for approaching these problems. The time has come for stocktaking and a review that will help in some way to a fuller development of liberation theology, which John Paul II describes as "not only timely but useful and necessary" (*Message*, no. 5). Liberation theology must look for correct answers that will be "as effective and constructive as possible and, at the same time, consistent and coherent with the teachings of the gospel, of the living tradition and of the ongoing magisterium of the church" (ibid.).[4]

During these years not all the participants in the discussion had equal knowledge of the situation and of the writings and reflections being discussed; the result was the confusions to which I referred. But amid the underbrush a more substantive process was at work, a process of serious and respectful confrontation, justified objections and legitimate submission of doubts, necessary clarification of points, and calm examination of the context of assertions that took on a different meaning there than when removed from connections that explained them. As a result of this process, the perspectives requiring further study became clearer, as did the work to be done.

To the people involved in this deeper and calmer discussion the recent Roman pronouncements (*LC* and *Message*) have therefore not come as a surprise; these documents are rather a sequel.[5] They do not withdraw condemnations, because there had been no condemnations; they do not represent compromises in the face of pressure or devices for avoiding divisions that in fact were never in sight.[6] Instead, as Cardinal Ratzinger said of the second instruction in the earlier mentioned interview, they are intended as "the point of departure for a new body of writings on the subject of Christian freedom and responsibility in the political and social spheres." He made it clear that the teaching of the magisterium "is not meant to replace the inquiries of theologians in this area, but simply to make clear the fixed points of reference, both biblical and anthropological, and their social consequences."[7] A new body of theological literature is justified by the emergence of new challenges.

The cardinal's words are an invitation to further reflection in this area. This will make it possible to settle some points and thereby move forward "in a positive way," with the help of the guidelines given, in the study and discernment of what both instructions look upon, in the language of John XXIII and the Council, as one of the major signs of the times in our age, the wish for liberation.[8]

It is in this spirit that I have tried to write the pages that follow.[9] I entertain the hope that they will help to shed light on some matters and make others better understood, to clear up certain misunderstandings and prevent possible ambiguities. Above all, it is my desire, as I take up old themes once again but along the new lines now opened up, to make clear my determination to serve the Lord, the church, and the people in the midst of whom it is my duty to bear witness to total liberation in Christ by proclaiming the kingdom of love and life. The connection between truth and freedom is emphasized in *LC* (it had already been emphasized, to some extent, in *LN*). Revealed truth must be made known to every human being; this is the starting point of every discourse on the faith. In the light of that truth it becomes possible to discern the Christian legitimacy of a particular praxis. The first part of the present essay will reflect on this decisive aspect of theological work.

The truth that makes us free is the Lord himself; the question of truth and freedom therefore turns our attention to the encounter between Christ, who is the truth of the Father, and human freedom.[10] Human freedom is historically conditioned

and undergoes historical transformations; an understanding of
the faith cannot dispense with analysis of these.[11] Moreover, the
discussion of these matters depends on the way in which salvation in Jesus Christ—that is, integral liberation—is understood. In the second part of the essay I intend to recall some
central aspects of this.

The first two parts will make it possible to take up, in the
third and last part, the subject of the church's mission. I shall
try to situate this mission in relation to the challenges of the
contemporary world and, in particular, the requirements of the
Latin American situation. One aspect of the mission is the social
dimension and the church's teaching in this area. But the theology of liberation does not confine itself to reflecting on that
area. As a theology centered on the mystery of Christ, it seeks
to go beyond requirements in the field of social justice.

For all the care I mean to exercise in giving accurate explanations that will clear up possible ambiguities and in rejecting
what I regard as mistaken interpretations of the topics discussed,
these pages will be simply a stage in a dialogue that must be
continued and carried further.[12]

LC says that "the words of Jesus, 'The truth will make you
free' (Jn. 8:32), must enlighten and guide all theological reflection and all pastoral decisions in this area" (no. 3). I therefore
take this text of the gospel as my guiding thread in the following
pages, but I am aware that I face a wide open task.[13]

TRUTH AND THEOLOGY

The primordial, and in a certain sense unique, source of
revealed truth is Jesus the Christ. The announcement of the
kingdom must be made to persons living in a particular historical
and cultural situation, but it takes on its full meaning only when
connected with Jesus, a man born of Mary and a participant in
human history, whom we acknowledge to be the Son who invites
us to a lasting, saving incarnation. The good news is Jesus Christ
himself. Any reflection on the truths of Christianity and on the
language needed for communicating them must start from him
who is the truth. Believing in the truth and putting it into practice are two necessary and mutually implicative aspects of the

following of Jesus, which is the obligatory setting of all theological reflection.

DIALOGUE WITH THE CONTEMPORARY MENTALITY

Theology is talk about God. Therefore, it derives its meaning from, and has its proper setting in, service of the church's proclamation of the gospel.[14] Every sound theology is inspired by a will to evangelization. This goal does not lessen its intellectual and critical demands, but it does give these their context and prevents theology from getting lost in marginal commentaries that keep it from saying the yes and no for which the gospel calls (see Mt. 5:37).

Faith and Culture

Theology's talk about God is addressed to concrete persons in order to make Jesus known to them or rekindle their faith in him or help them discern the ways in which they can give authentic obedience to his message. Such talk about God must therefore be intelligible to those who hear the message; it has its proper autonomy, which it derives from the revealed source (the scriptures as they live on in tradition), but it uses human words that have a particular historical and cultural setting. All references to revelation must use this mediation and with its help disclose the meaning of the Lord's living word and its demands upon the period through which we are passing.

If the proclamation of the message is to be an effective invitation to the following of Jesus, it must take as its springboard the experiences and questions of those who hear the word of God, as well as the mental categories that they use in trying to understand their experiences of life. Every theology is, and must be, a dialogue with the culture of its age. The dialogue brings into play the theology's capacity for making the gospel relevant in human history. This supposes, on the one hand, a lucid fidelity to the "deposit of faith" and, on the other, a great loyalty to the historical moment in which theology is being developed.

Permanently valid in this area is the example given by the Greek fathers, Augustine, and Thomas Aquinas, among those of long ago, and of Karl Barth and Karl Rahner among our contemporaries (to mention only those who are no longer with us).

An understanding of the faith that does not start from the way the gospel is lived in today's church, especially by the poor in the form of basic ecclesial communities, will be leaving aside a fundamental datum of our faith—namely, the life of the church as a *locus theologicus*. If it loses sight of the subject who lives and reflects, it will also fail to exercise its social function.[15]

A Latin American theology that prescinds from the unjust suffering—with all its demands and challenges—of the majority of our peoples cannot speak of God and expect to be heard.[16] At another level, a theology that does not take into account the shifts in rational categories that are occurring in today's world runs the risk of expressing itself in a language alien to its age and of thereby failing in its duty of presenting the message to that age.

In dealing with this third aspect it is necessary also to take into account the influence of the sciences (both the exact sciences and the "human" sciences) on human knowledge. For centuries, human knowledge followed the path of philosophical speculation. The appearance on the scene of physics, and later of biology, represented a first challenge to this single model of knowing, for these sciences laid the emphasis on experimentation and claimed to be able to alter the natural world. Philosophy felt the impact, and its most far-sighted representatives frequented the world of the sciences (Descartes, Malebranche, Leibniz, Hume, Kant).

The nineteenth century saw the birth of a further effort to understand such complex fields as history and the life of the psyche by applying scientific principles. Because the terrain here is so difficult, these endeavors have not taken more than their first steps; a further difficulty is that they are looking for a scientific approach that will not be simply an imitation (something that in any case is impossible) of what is done in the world of physics.[17]

These new disciplines had a major impact on knowledge of a philosophical (and theological) type, despite their inchoative character, because they deal with very sensitive aspects of the human person. "The advent of the social and psychological sciences extended this type of knowledge, in a way, to areas hitherto reserved to considerations of a philosophical type. These are the sciences that, preserving their internal character as theoretical sciences, tend at the same time to become 'humane sciences' " (*Power*, p. 58). There is certainly no question of letting the human sciences replace philosophy, which retains all its value in the work of theology; the point rather is to take into account the complexity of human knowing. "Reason has, especially today, many other manifestations than philosophical ones" (*Liberation*, p. 5).

One result of this process has been the gradual appearance of an important trait of the contemporary mentality: knowledge is seen as increasingly tied up with action. In saying this, I am obviously not throwing out other dimensions of human knowledge but simply emphasizing something that has emerged in recent times. This perception of the link between knowledge and action makes even more challenging the questions raised about situations of injustice and the marginalization of human rights, especially those of the poorest. In this area a type of knowledge has made its appearance that can help to transform a state of affairs offensive to human dignity.

Theory and Practice

This entire development has thrown into relief the practical aspects of knowledge and thus revived a traditional topic of human reflection: the distinction between theory and practice. As everyone knows, the distinction comes to us from Greek thought.

The theme is to be found in Pythagoras, but it takes clearer shape in Aristotle. In his *Nicomachean Ethics* the philosopher distinguishes between political activity and the life of contemplation. The former is characteristic of persons of action and is signified by the word "praxis"; the latter is the life of the mind, dedicated to the knowledge of eternal truths. Contemplation (theory) ranks higher than praxis,[18] but both are dimensions of human existence.

This distinction and the relation between its two terms would henceforth influence Greek philosophy, but in different ways. Plotinus, for example, would place the emphasis on theory inso-

far as this means union with God to the disparagement of political praxis. This position in turn would influence theology, where
theory would be thought of as contemplation and union with
God, and practice would be seen primarily as work for the neighbor, or the active life. The early centuries of Christianity continued to assert the primacy of the contemplative life. Later on,
however, the rise of the mendicant orders led Thomas Aquinas
to propose the superiority of the "mixed life," which starts with
contemplation but aims ultimately to communicate the fruits of
contemplation to others, *contemplata aliis tradere.*

Duns Scotus was the first in the Middle Ages to revive the
Greek word "praxis" and to ask: "What is praxis?" In his view,
God is also an object of practical knowledge. This was not yet
the modern meaning of praxis; because of his well known vol-
untarism, however, Duns Scotus did attach high value to the
practical aspects of everyday life.

I have already spoken of the rise of the experimental sciences
in the sixteenth century. For our purposes here, I must add
Macchiavelli's effort to think of the political order as a world
possessing its own rationality and even a certain autonomy in
relation to ethico-religious principles. Both factors—the sciences above all, but also politics—led to a philosophical outlook
that emphasizes the activity of the knowing subject.[19]

Against this background, Kant takes the position that while
theoretical reason can raise and answer the question "What can
I know?" it cannot answer the question "What ought I to do?"
Only practical reason can answer this second question; in addition, it, and it alone, deals with the central problems: God, freedom, and the immortality of the soul. These subjects elude the
grip of theoretical reason, which can only end up in aporias
(contradictory statements) when it tackles them. Here, in the
setting of an idealist philosophy, we see a turn toward practice,
which, in this case, is the moral life. As Hegel was to say later
on, Kant reveals his stature more fully in the *Critique of Practical
Reason* than in the *Critique of Pure Reason.*

The theme of theory and praxis is also present in Hegel, who
focuses his attention on history as the unfolding and assertion
of human freedom, but it is even clearer in some of his followers.
One of these, August Cieszkowski, a Polish Catholic, makes

praxis the final stage of philosophical thought; only in that stage are the classic antinomies of philosophy resolved.[20]

A significant milepost on this journey is the undeniably important contribution that Marx made in his effort at a scientific understanding of history. The polemical and caustic tone of this contribution has so affected some that in their view anything having to do with "theory and praxis" must be immediately labeled "Marxist." As a matter of fact, however, while allowing for both the continuity and the breaks characteristic of the history of ideas, we must say that when we speak of "theory and praxis" we are dealing with a very ancient tradition of Western philosophy, one that has taken on new life due to the challenges of the experimental sciences and to a different view of the political world.

Whatever the role played by the development I have described, the fact is that the modern mind is more alert today than in the past to the practical impact of knowledge. It is not satisfied with general claims but looks for some kind of verification that is connected with everyday life and especially with the transformation of human — or, rather, infrahuman — situations, which it rejects for ethical and religious reasons.

This trait of contemporary consciousness is one that theologians cannot ignore. As we shall see further on, the importance attributed to practice in Christian life is due chiefly to factors of a theological and spiritual kind. This does not mean that we are to take over, in its rough form and unchanged, the idea of praxis to be found in particular schools of thought; the issue rather is to be attentive to the complexity of an evolution and to the form in which it has penetrated the culture of our age and become there a common patrimony. There is need also of being alert to past connections, including the influence of Christian thought on the historical development of the idea. Involved here is an important aspect of Christianity's dialogue with modern culture and its effort to bring the Christian message to those who live in that culture.

Nonetheless — and this must be kept clear — there is no authentic dialogue unless each side has an identity of its own; dialogue supposes a relation between two persons or mentalities. For this reason, it is not enough to be alert to what is characteristic of present-day thought; any coming to grips with it or any approach to other positions is possible only through recourse to our own sources.[21] These sources have not yet yielded up all their riches, for we always approach them in terms of our own questions and experiences; but we ought to approach them chiefly with a willingness to accept their challenges and the changes they may call for in our life and our thinking.[22]

The need of making the gospel message heard not only does not excuse, but even requires, theology to enter more deeply into that which plays the decisive role in it: the primacy of the word. It is by its fidelity to this norm that the value of any understanding of the faith within the church will finally be assessed, for the truth of any understanding of the faith is rooted in that fidelity.[23] For the truth consists in obedience to Christ, the center of our faith. "The primacy of God and the grace of faith give theological work its raison d'être."[24]

BETWEEN PROMISE AND FULFILLMENT

In some Christian circles the word "truth" almost immediately conveys the meaning given to it in traditional philosophy of Greek origin. According to that philosophy, truth resides in the essences of things, and we reach it via the connection that exists between any given thing and the idea we construct of it; if there is conformity between reality and idea, we possess the truth about the thing. This is a legitimate, intellectual approach that many regard as typical of the Greek world.[25] It has left its impress on the history of Western philosophy.

Biblical Truth

The Semitic mentality, which is that of the Bible, has a very different conception of truth.[26] The Hebrew word translated as "truth" (namely, *'emet* and related words, from which comes our "amen") implies solidity, fidelity, reliability, trustworthiness. The perspective here is concrete and historical; it reflects the world of the interpersonal, where what happens is as important as, or even more important than, what is.

More specifically: truth in the scriptures is a relation not between things and concepts but between promise and fulfillment. This relation is so basic that some have thought to see in it the central theme around which it would be possible to construct a theology of the Old Testament and even of the entire Bible. Be that as it may, it is certain that the dialectic of promise and fulfillment has a direct reference to God. It situates us in the context of a relation between persons and not between things and concepts. It points to God being revealed in history through the fulfillment of God's promise of love and redemption. Promise and fulfillment serve as it were as the broad arch within which are located the Old Testament idea of the covenant and the establishment of the new covenant by Jesus.[27]

From the Christian viewpoint, this relation reveals the deeper meaning of human history, which it constantly raises, as it were, above itself.[28] For the fulfillment of the promise is not completed in the historical process: "The promise is gradually revealed in all its universality and concrete expression: it is *already* fulfilled in historical events, but *not yet* completely; it incessantly projects itself into the future, creating a permanent historical mobility."[29]

In the Bible, God is called trustworthy because God does what God proposes, because God is faithful to God's promise and people. Psalm 89 says as much: "I will sing of thy steadfast love, O Lord, forever; with my mouth I will proclaim thy faithfulness to all generations. For thy steadfast love was established forever, thy faithfulness is firm as the heavens" (vv. 1–2). God does not withdraw a promise: "The Lord swore to David a sure oath from which he will not turn back: 'One of the sons of your body I will set on your throne' " (Ps. 132:11). This unshakable steadfastness of God is what rouses and creates faith or *pistis*, that is, confidence in and surrender to God. God's fidelity to God's promises stimulates, and passes judgment on, our fidelity.

The biblical idea of truth reaches its full depth of meaning in this relation between promise and fulfillment.[30] For this reason, the element of time, of achievement through the historical process, plays an important role in the idea of truth as seen by the Bible. Kasper writes: "The Hebrew idea of truth has a specifically historical character. . . . Truth must be verified in time, in the sequence of events."[31]

"I Am the Truth"

The promise issuing from the Father's love is fulfilled in a sovereign and unparalleled way in Jesus the Christ. When Jesus says "I am the truth" (Jn. 14:6), he is saying: in me the Father's promise is fulfilled.[32] John also tells us in his gospel: "God so loved the world that he gave his only Son" (3:16). In this sending, in the Word made human flesh, a promise is fulfilled. God is revealed as trustworthy through the sending of Jesus: "He who sent me is true" (Jn. 8:26) — that is, faithful and worthy of credence and self-surrender.

In all this, we are speaking, of course, of the way we approach God and understand God's fidelity to us. In Scholastic terms, our viewpoint is *quoad nos*. But the Bible also vigorously emphasizes God's transcendence and speaks of God independently of God's action in history; it adopts, again in Scholastic terms, the *quoad se* viewpoint. For we may never forget that "the God revealed in history is a God irreducible to our manner of understanding, to our theology, even to our faith itself. It is impossible to appropriate to oneself this God who becomes present in events, this God who becomes history. ... God is the utterly Other, the Holy One."[33]

As Gerhard von Rad remarks, "it is in history that God reveals the secret of his person."[34] Both aspects have to be preserved: our access to God through God's saving action in history, and the transcendent mystery of God's presence:

> It is certain that we know the Lord through the Lord's works, but these very works reveal to us that God delivers because God is a liberator, that God enters into agreements because God is faithful, that God does justice because God is justice, and not the converse, as we tend to think. God sanctifies because God is holy; God gives life because he is Life, because God is who God is. This is certainly the sense of Yahweh's self-description to Moses: "I am who I am."[35]

Because God is who and what God is, God gives life, saves, and so on; because God is truth, God is revealed as trustworthy. The approach to the mystery of God is always a complex process and one that is, to a large extent, full of surprises.

The God who is "Wholly Other" (to use Karl Barth's expression) comes to meet us through the incarnation of the Son. If we accept the historical testimony of the actions and words of Jesus, we can attain to the Father: "He who has seen me has seen the Father" (Jn. 14:9). Jesus is the way, apart from which there is no access to the Father and to the life that comes from him. God sent the Son "that whoever believes in him should not perish but have eternal life" (Jn. 3:16). In Jesus Christ, who is the full and unexpected fulfillment of the Father's promise, history and eschatology are tied together, the present and the ultimate meaning of time. All this is expressed in the words, "I am the truth." Jesus Christ is the first and last word, the alpha and the omega, the beginning and the end (Rv. 22:13).

The starting point of Christian life and therefore of theology is the encounter with Christ, in whom we recognize God to be love and Father, and other human beings to be our brothers and sisters. The truth that liberates is Christ himself and his every action and word.

THE FOLLOWING OF JESUS

Christian life is, above all else, a *sequela Christi*, a following of Christ. The proper doing of theology (the method, the way) has its place within this movement (itself a way) toward the Father.

Jesus calls himself the truth, but he also describes himself as the way and the life (see Jn. 14:6). His actions and words, his practice, show us the course to follow.[36] The Lord proclaims a truth that must be put into practice; that is why works are regarded as so important throughout the New Testament. Passages to this effect abound, and there is no point in giving a list of them.

Doing the Truth

The Gospel of John, which is so concerned with the connection between truth and freedom, contains a passage that is especially interesting: "This is the judgment, that the light has come into the world, and men loved darkness rather than light, because their deeds were evil. For everyone who does evil hates the light, and does not come to the light, lest his deeds should be exposed. But he who does what is true comes to the light, that it may be clearly seen that his deeds have been wrought by God" (Jn. 3:19–21). The passage pulls together some central themes of this gospel. The judgment passed on some is based on their rejection of the light, "because their deeds were evil." "Doing the truth," on the other hand, means accepting the light—that is, Christ and his word, and therefore doing deeds that are in accord with God.

The truth that the Lord reveals to us "is done" or "practiced" in the activity of the disciple who thus welcomes the gift of the word. Paul Tillich brings out nicely the reason for this: "Truth is something new, something done by God in history and therefore something done in the life of each person."[37] This line of thought leads to the theme of verification by praxis. The process described in the section, some pages back, on the idea of praxis, can stimulate our attention to this outlook; it is natural, and has often happened in the history of theology, that an element of contemporary culture should make us especially sensitive to some aspect of the Christian message. But the power and meaning of "doing the truth" come first and foremost from the Bible itself.

Karl Lehmann rightly says that "Christian faith cannot dispense with proving itself in deeds."[38] The importance of this verification in the realm of deeds has been frequently emphasized in the teaching of the present pope, John Paul II. In his encyclical *On Human Work* (*Laborem Exercens*; henceforth *LE*) he has this carefully worded statement: "Hence in every case a just wage is the concrete means of *verifying* the justice of the whole socioeconomic system and, in any case, of *checking* that it is functioning justly. It is not the only means of *checking*, but it is a particularly important one and in a sense the key means" (*LE* 19; italics added).[39] At a more ecclesiological level, and in connection with movements of solidarity among workers, the pope maintains that "the church is firmly committed to this cause for she considers it her mission, her service, a *proof* of her fidelity to Christ, so that she can truly be the 'church of the poor' " (*LE*, 8; italics added).

Does this perhaps mean that faith is reduced to works? Not at all! The contemplative dimension is an essential element of Christian life. Faith, however, must be translated into deeds;

otherwise it is a dead faith (Jm. 2:17).[40] At the same time, as St. Paul vigorously reminds us, deeds or works do not save by themselves. Salvation is a gift, an expression of the unmerited and freely given love of God. But the two themes converge and call for one another without being confused with one another: if we must "do the truth," the reason is that truth here is a saving truth,[41] a truth that is active in history and life.

What has been said makes it possible to situate properly the concept of praxis, to which contemporary theology frequently appeals[42] and which plays an important role in liberation theology. It involves a transformative activity that is influenced and illumined by Christian love. *A Theology of Liberation* has a section entitled "Historical Praxis," which lists the various factors that have led to emphasis on this aspect in our time. They are as follows: "Charity has been rediscovered as the center of the Christian life" (more specifically: it is "the foundation of the praxis of Christians, of their active presence in history"); the evolution of Christian spirituality; a greater sensitivity "to the anthropological aspects of revelation"; "the very life of the church" seen as a *locus theologicus*; Blondel's view of "human action as the point of departure for all reflection"; "the influence of Marxist thought," as a result of which "theological thought, searching for its own sources, has begun to reflect on the meaning of the transformation of this world"; and finally the rediscovery of the eschatological dimension. These eight factors have led to recognition of "the work and importance of concrete behavior, of deeds, of action, of praxis in the Christian life." Six of the factors are theological in nature, and two (Blondel and Marx) are philosophical.[43]

A lengthy passage which I wrote a few years ago clarified this point still further by applying a synthetic view of the idea of praxis. I think it worth citing here:

What is really at stake . . . is not simply a greater rationality in economic activity, or a better social organization, but, over and above all this, justice and love. To be sure, these classic concepts do not often come up in the language of political science. But there is no avoiding them here. And this demonstrates the human depth and density of the matter with which we are dealing.

The use of the terms "justice" and "love" recalls to our minds that we are speaking of real human persons, whole peoples, suffering misery and exploitation, deprived of the most elemental human rights, scarcely aware that they are human beings at all. The praxis of liberation, therefore, inasmuch as it starts out from an authentic solidarity with the poor and the oppressed, is ultimately a praxis of love — real love, effective and concrete, for real, concrete human beings. It is a praxis of love of neighbor, and of love for Christ in the neighbor, for Christ identifies himself with the least of these human beings, our brothers and sisters. Any attempt to separate love for God and love for neighbor gives rise to attitudes that impoverish both.

It is easy to make a distinction between a heavenly and an earthly praxis — easy, but not faithful to the gospel of the Word who became a human being. It therefore would seem more authentic and profound to speak of a praxis of love as having its roots in the gratuitous and free love of the Father and as becoming concrete in solidarity with human beings — first with the poor and dispossessed, and then through them with all human beings.[44]

Liberating praxis, which is, in the final analysis, a praxis of love, is thus based, without reductionism of any kind, on the gratuitousness of God's love. It brings us, through solidarity with the poor and oppressed, into solidarity with every human being.

Orthodoxy and Orthopraxis

In relation to praxis theology exercises a critical function "in the light of faith" (*Liberation*, passim). This reference to the classical *lumen fidei* means that the critical reflection is not philosophical or sociological but theological. As Karl Lehmann remarks, faith "cannot be unqualifiedly identified with any type of praxis" (*Problems*, p. 25). Discernment is needed, and therefore recourse to the sources of revelation, for it is from the latter that the applicable criteria must be derived. As the Peruvian bishops put it:

For Christians the supreme norms of truth in ethical and religious matters are to be found in revelation as interpreted by those legitimately empowered to do so. Every theology must have its basis in revelation, in the deposit of faith. With this as a foundation it is possible to reflect on anything and everything, including praxis, which always remains subordinate to revelation [*Documento*, no. 44].

The ultimate criteria come from revealed truth, which we accept in faith and not from praxis itself. It is meaningless—it would, among other things, be a tautology—to say that praxis is to be criticized "in the light of praxis." Moreover, to take such an approach would in any case be to cease doing properly theological work. I think it important to assert this very clearly in order to clear up any ambiguities that the emphasis on the value of practice might produce in some minds.[45]

The perspective thus adopted in liberation theology has been well understood by P. Vanzan, who writes as follows of the liberation theologians in the authoritative journal, *La Civiltà Cattolica:*

These theologians have in fact a profound awareness that praxis is not normative of itself: it can become ambiguous and perverted if it departs from the norms of the gospel. For this reason, in the liberation theology of Gutiérrez and the other authors mentioned above, the word of God and the teaching of the church ensure the "Christian" character of a praxis, while liberating praxis in turn ensures that the Christian truth and the faith of the Church are faithful to history and are being translated into practice by bringing life, and even abundant life, to all levels and every area (to paraphrase Jn. 10:10 in the light of *Populorum Progressio*).[46]

This carefully worded passage clearly brings out the role of praxis in theological reflection on it, reflection that is first and foremost an understanding of the faith.

For this reason, and also in order to avoid being too abstract, we must keep in mind that the criterion used in discernment comes from a faith that is lived and shared in the communion of the church. By this I mean, as I noted above, a faith that necessarily leads to concrete actions of love for neighbor, or, to put it differently, a faith that necessarily inspires a practice. Thus understood, it also helps us perceive aspects of the Christian message that would otherwise be hidden from us. The 1984 Instruction can therefore say:

> Likewise the experience of those who work directly for evangelization and for the advancement of the poor and the oppressed is necessary for the doctrinal and pastoral reflection of the church. In this sense it is necessary to affirm that one becomes more aware of certain aspects of truth by starting with praxis, if by that one means pastoral praxis and social work that keeps its evangelical inspiration [*LN*, XI, 13].

The "deposit of faith" is not a set of cold, warehoused truths but, on the contrary, lives on in the church, where it stimulates types of behavior that are faithful to the Lord's will, calls for its proclamation, and provides criteria for discernment in relation to the world in which the church finds itself.

A great deal still remains to be learned about revealed truth;[47] we have not exhausted its wealth of meaning. The 1988 Instruction says, therefore, that "a theological reflection developed from a particular experience can constitute a very positive contribution, inasmuch as it makes possible a highlighting of aspects of the word of God, the richness of which had not yet been fully grasped" (*LC*, no. 70). Revealed truth is life; hence the importance of ecclesial experience, as the same Instruction carefully states in a passage heavy with fruitful implications:

> But in order that this reflection may be truly a reading of the scripture and not a projection onto the word of God of a meaning it does not contain, theologians will be careful to interpret the experience from which they begin *in the light of the experience of the church itself*. This experience of the church shines with a singular brightness and in all its purity in the lives of the saints. It pertains to the pastors

of the church, in communion with the successor of Peter,
to discern its authenticity [ibid.; italics added].

It is significant that this passage speaks of "the light of the
experience of the church." A kind of intellectualism has caused
many to distrust giving Christian experience a role in theological
work, perhaps because they unduly oppose experience and the
affirmation of truth. In fact, Christian truths need to be lived if
they are to be stated correctly and in a more than superficial
way. The experience of the church extends to the Christian message — that is, the deposit of faith; the message, the deposit, have
their place in the people of God journeying to the Father. The
reference to the saints, the very persons who have lived the
teachings of Jesus and put them into practice in a higher way,
is especially a stimulant to theological work.[48]

Critical reflection "in the light of the word"[49] is only one
function of theology (the others are theology as wisdom and
theology as rationally organized knowledge),[50] but it makes it
possible properly to situate the relation between orthodoxy and
orthopraxis, which has been so debated and is so open to misunderstandings and erroneous interpretations.

The emphasis on correct behavior or orthopraxis has polemical overtones when set over against an attitude that gives an
almost exclusively privileged place to the doctrinal aspect (or
what an intellectualist approach sometimes takes to be the doctrinal aspect) of the Christian message.[51] This attitude undeniably exists, and both the magisterium and contemporary
theology have referred to it, even before Vatican II but especially since, given the council's stress on concrete Christian life.
The critique of that attitude was occasioned by the imbalance
it introduced into the living of the gospel. There is no doubt, of
course, that the earlier mentioned emphasis of the contemporary mind on the practical aspects of human knowledge has
played a part in creating the new sensitivity to orthopraxis. At
the same time, however, this new sensitivity represents a revival
of perspectives that have always had a place in the Christian
community.

It is important also to observe that in liberation theology the
subject of orthopraxis is studied in the context of the role played

by eschatology in contemporary theology. The setting is important, because this perspective opens us "to the gift that gives
history its transcendent meaning: the full and definitive encounter with the Lord and with other humans" (*Liberation*, p. 8). The
emphasis on historical practice is therefore directly connected
with the Christian affirmation of a world beyond the present
life.

The purpose in thus stressing the importance of orthopraxis
is to throw into relief the role in Christian life of concrete commitment along the lines of that "doing of the truth" that we saw
a few pages back. It should be clear that this is not at all to deny
"the meaning of orthodoxy, understood as a proclamation of
and reflection on statements considered to be true" (ibid.).
Right thinking is essential for believers who have received the
faith within the church.

The challenge is to be able to preserve the circular relationship between orthodoxy and orthopraxis and the nourishment
of each by the other. Light is cast on this matter by Mark 8:27–
35, a key passage, where the confession of faith in the messiah
and the practical following of him imply one another.[52] As Paul
Tillich says, "Christian theology is rooted in a concept of truth
in which there can be no separation between theory and practice, because this truth is saving truth" (*Shaking of the Foundations*, p. 117).

Especially meaningful in regard to Christian freedom is the
context of the statement that Christ is the truth that sets us free
(Jn. 8:32). This context shows that to be free means: to be a
disciple (v. 31), to know the truth (v. 32), not to be self-sufficient
(v. 33), not to be a slave to sin (v. 35), to be a child of God (v.
35), and to receive the word (v. 36).

Christian praxis derives its meaning from the following of
Jesus, from the practice of the Lord himself.[53] Encounter with
Christ is the point of departure for our faith in ecclesial communion and for our understanding of it. Jesus Christ is the hermeneutical principle for all understanding of the faith:

> In Jesus we encounter God. In the human word we read
> the word of the Lord. In the events of history we recognize
> the fulfillment of the promise. And all this because Jesus

is the Christ of God, the one sent by the Father: the Son.
"Yes, God loved the world so much that he gave his only
Son" (Jn. 3:16).

For Jesus is the irruption into history of the one by
whom everything was made and everything was saved.
This, then, is the fundamental hermeneutical circle: from
humanity to God and from God to humanity, from history
to faith and from faith to history, from the human word to
the word of the Lord and from the word of the Lord to
the human word, from the love of one's brothers and sisters to the love of the Father and from the love of the
Father to love of one's brothers and sisters, from human
justice to God's holiness and from God's holiness to human
justice.

Theology — the understanding of the faith — is animated
by the will to help others live according to the Spirit
[*Power*, p. 61].

The truth that the understanding of the faith aims to enter
into more deeply and to know with all its demands upon believers is Jesus Christ himself. He is the supreme norm of theological discourse to the same extent that he is the supreme norm
of our entire life. The indispensable condition for a correct
reflection on faith, which is God's gift, is that we make his practice our own, make his way in history ours, and love as he loved
us.

THE WAY OF LIBERATION

Christ is the truth, a truth that sets us free. The liberation
he gives is an integral one that embraces all dimensions of
human existence and brings us to full communion with God and
one another. This liberation is therefore one that begins within
history, which thus becomes a way to a fullness that lies beyond
it.

An examination of the historical changes in the idea of freedom will bring to light their different perspectives on God and
the poor. In this area, the basic datum of our faith is Christ's
lordship over the development of the human race, a truth of

which St. Paul was especially conscious. This basic datum enables us to understand that liberation — within which we can distinguish different levels — is a journey toward communion.
Communion, however, is a gift of Christ who sets us free in order
that we may be free, free to love; it is in this communion that
full freedom resides (see Gal. 5:1 and 13).

FAR FROM GOD . . . AND FROM THE POOR

The second (1986) Instruction begins with an interesting discussion and critique of the European movement toward the various freedoms characteristic of the modern age. This phase of
history is heavy with consequences for that continent and the
contemporary world generally, as well as for the task of the
church in our time. It is important to recall the main lines of
this stage of European history and bring to light the ruptures
taking place in the poor countries in relation to this development.

The Movement for the Modern Freedoms
The question of human freedom has always been a challenge
to the Christian conscience. Christianity preaches a truth that
saves, and this truth must be accepted by free beings. Truth and
freedom thus stand in a fruitful tension. Christian life is a dialogue between a God who calls and human beings who respond;
their response must be free, just as the gift is free that God
wants to make of God's self.

Truth and Freedom. The question of freedom arose even in
the first centuries. Faced with the hostility of the Roman
Empire, which sought to impose its will, Christians firmly
claimed the rights they associated with their religious faith. They
found the ultimate basis for this claim in sacred scripture, but
the historical situation in which they were living made them
keenly, and increasingly, conscious of it. Tertullian and Lactantius are the two great witnesses from this period. Both clearly
assert that freedom of religion is a right of every human being
and that political authorities have no jurisdiction in this area.
Both of these assertions are based on a profound conviction —

namely, that freedom is a condition for attaining to truth.[54]

From the fourth century on, the situation of Christianity in the empire changed. The basic insights in the matter of religious freedom lost something of their urgency, for a new factor now had to be taken into account: the existence of a political authority that placed itself at the service of the Christian religion. True enough, the essential point in the claim of religious freedom persisted, but it took a different form. The claim now was that the act of faith is free; in other words, any imposition of Christian truth was rejected; no one could be forced to accept the faith.[55] This was a problem unknown to the earlier centuries when Christianity was being persecuted in the Roman Empire. The very fact that the new question could be raised shows that the historical situation of Christianity had indeed changed. There was an even greater change from the earlier refusal to allow political authorities any competence in religious matters. From the sixth century on, the emphasis was rather on the service that the temporal power should render to religious truth, although this service ought never take the form of imposing the faith.[56] This ministerial conception of political power in relation to religion was to be reaffirmed throughout the Middle Ages, to the extent, at times, of seriously endangering freedom in these matters.

The question of religious freedom was posed anew in connection with the Protestant Reformation and Renaissance humanism. But, as *Libertatis Conscientia* says, "it was above all in the age of the Enlightenment and at the French Revolution that the call to freedom rang out with full force" (no. 6). The call was for freedom for the human person in various areas, one of these — and a very important one — being the area of religion. Down to our own day, modernity, with its lights and shadows, has influenced European society and has had repercussions in other parts of the world.

Everyone is aware of the attitude of rejection that the church adopted toward this movement for the modern freedoms. If we read the documents of the popes from Pius VI to Pius IX, it is easy to see that a single major concern, expressed in different ways, motivated rejection: persuasion that these freedoms would endanger the salvation of human beings. According to these documents, the removal of Catholicism from its position as the religion of the state and the proclamation of civil equality for other forms of worship are the results of an indifferentism that puts truth and error on the same level.

The confrontation that went on throughout the nineteenth century was to be painful and abrasive for the church. Its institutional influence decreased in European society. The confrontation occurred in Latin America, as well, although to a lesser degree. On the other hand, with the passage of time the elements that initially seemed to form a monolithic block were separated out. Needed distinctions were gradually made, misunderstandings were cleared up, and the representatives of both liberalism and the church came to speak more calmly. It came to be realized that many claims of modernity had a Christian source. Some Christian circles ("liberal Catholicism") accepted the new perspectives, rejecting the charge that they could be in opposition to their faith.[57] Their attitude was one of magnanimity and readiness for dialogue; this did not, however, exclude the ambivalence to be seen in every historical process. Their position, though vigorously rejected by the popes in the beginning (cf. the condemnations of Gregory XVI and Pius IX), has been enriched with new perspectives and has gradually been spreading.

The position taken by the popes gradually changed during the twentieth century; then came Vatican II. The "Declaration on Religious Freedom," which is often cited in the first chapter of *Libertatis Conscientia*, was one of the most keenly debated documents of the council, for the burden of the bitter and painful discussion that had gone on for over a century was still too great to cast aside easily. The so-called conciliar minority believed that to defend religious freedom would be to undermine the papal magisterium of the previous century. The victory finally went, however, to the principle that distinguishes between the legitimacy of the demand for modern freedoms, especially religious freedom, and the ideological and antireligious wrappings in which the claim was initially made by some.

Distance from God. Libertatis Conscientia adopts the perspective of the "Declaration on Religious Freedom" and fervently defends religious freedom and other human freedoms. The Instruction honestly acknowledges the "errors of judgment and serious omissions for which Christians have been responsible in the course of the centuries" (no. 20) in this area. There were indeed errors and omissions. We have mentioned only what happened with the matter of religious freedom, but there are other cases.

These mistakes inflicted a great deal of suffering; above all, however, they were an obstacle to the vital presence of the gospel in today's world. Much of what we now criticize in modern society is due to the fact that we Christians could not be lucidly involved in its construction, attentive to what is valid in its demands, and able to share our own message. History has taught us a painful but rewarding lesson here. We should therefore welcome with joy the resolute defense in *Libertatis Conscientia* of religious freedom and of human freedoms generally.

The greatest mistake was to think that the assertion of religious freedom would be at the expense of Christian truth. Truth and error were hypostasized, and it was said that truth alone has rights, when in fact only the human person is a subject of rights over against the civil power. The Christians of the first centuries realized from experience and reflection that truth and freedom were not opposed, that the latter was the necessary condition for attaining the former. Their historical context made this vision of things easier for the early Christians; our task is to renew the vision in our own situation, which is evidently much more complex.

The conciliar "Declaration on Religious Freedom" takes this point into account and begins with a resolute affirmation regarding the truth that saves (no. 1, a text based on a draft edited by Yves Congar), in order then to maintain, no less resolutely, that "the human person has a right to religious freedom" (no. 2). The council does not go into the theological difficulties of the subject but provides what might be called a necessary mental hygiene in regard to it and prepares the way for entering more deeply into it.[58]

Libertatis Conscientia vigorously defends the permanent values of religious freedom as well as its present necessity in face of the totalitarian threats in today's world. The present situation causes the Vatican Congregation to review the history of recent centuries with its successes,[59] but also with its errors that still prevail today.[60] The situation also allows the Congregation to review the relation between the church and freedom. While acknowledging past "errors of judgment," it asserts, with good reason, that much of the church's criticism of the modern world "has often been misunderstood. ... With the passage of time, however, it is possible to do greater justice to the church's point of view" (no. 20).

The 1988 Instruction has some relevant remarks on this reaction of the modern world, and it criticizes as unacceptable the opposition that some facets of the modern mentality set up between God and the human person: "For many ... , it is God who is the specific alienation of humankind. There is said to be a radical incompatibility between the affirmation of God and of human freedom. By rejecting belief in God, they say, humankind will become truly free" (no. 18). Unbelief or skepticism in religious matters and distance from God are in fact characteristic of important areas of modern consciousness.

The Ambiguities of a Process

The intellectual and philosophical side of the movement for modern freedoms—the movement we know as the Enlightenment—set goals and raised aspirations that very soon began to be disappointed. The initial optimism quickly faded. The most clearsighted representatives of the movement saw the internal contradictions in the process they themselves were promoting. Hegel could already speak of the "unsatisfied Enlightenment."[61] From the very first decades of the period, people were also aware of the paradoxical possibility of totalitarianism in the assertion of freedoms.[62]

Modern Individualism. Libertatis Conscientia takes up and continues this criticism first made from within the historical process that went on mainly in Europe but also found acceptance in certain intellectual and political minorities in Latin America. Apart from its consequences in the area of religion, this criticism is the line followed in the position that the document takes in regard to the present phase in the history of the

Western world, a phase known as modernity and having its own claims in the areas of reason and freedom. *Libertatis Conscientia* aptly says that "in the field of social and political achievements, one of the fundamental ambiguities of the affirmation of freedom in the age of the Enlightenment had to do with the concept of the subject of this freedom as an individual who is fully self-sufficient and whose finality is the satisfaction of its own interests in the enjoyment of earthly goods" (no. 13).

In fact, the chief characteristic of the modern mentality is its radical individualism. In the area of economics this outlook finds clear expression in the declaration of human rights as enunciated by the French revolution: "Every man is free to use his muscles, his skills, and his capital as appears good and useful to himself. He can make what pleases him and what seems good to him." There is no other objective than one's own will and interests. This outlook gave rise to an exaggerated view of the legitimate right of private property as the setting in which responsible personal freedom was to be exercised. A liberal historian has rightly said: "Freedom in work is a child of modern individualism and even its favorite child."[63]

The individual is a first principle not only in economic activity but also in the building of society, for society is simply the sum total of the individual decisions that establish what J. J. Rousseau called a "social contract." The life of society is thus entirely in the hands of individuals and their interests. The viewpoint of the common good seems to carry less weight in social life.

Radical individualism also crops up in the area of knowledge. Nothing is to be accepted as true that has not been submitted to the judgment of critical reason. The mind of the individual is sovereign and acknowledges no higher authority in the economic world and even in social life.[64]

Radical individualism is the expression of the self-sufficiency which *Libertatis Conscientia* criticizes. We must recognize the existence of this individualism if we are to understand the contribution but also the tremendous limitations of the modern mentality. If we keep it in mind, we will not be surprised at what *Libertatis Conscientia* has to say about the situation created in the poor countries during the period of history in which the countries guided by social groups representative of the modern ideology were growing ever richer. The 1988 Instruction says that the individualist ideology "favored the unequal distribution of wealth at the beginning of the industrial era to the point that workers found themselves excluded from access to the essential goods that they had helped to produce and to which they had a right. Hence the birth of powerful liberation movements from the poverty caused by industrial society" (no. 13).[65]

The Underside of History. The point made in the 1986 Instruction is important; here again, however, it is necessary to go deeper and develop further the critique of the modern mentality. This will help to understand a theology done from "the underside of history."

In his encyclical on human work (*Laborem Exercens*; henceforth *LE*) John Paul II speaks as follows of the social consequences of the modern mentality: "In the modern period, from the beginning of the industrial age, the Christian truth about work had to oppose the various trends of *materialistic* and *economistic* thought" (no. 7, italics added). As a result of these trends, capital took precedence over labor. The pope goes on to speak of what happened as a consequence of the industrial age:

> It was precisely one such wide-ranging anomaly that gave rise in the last century to what has been called "the worker question," sometimes described as "the proletariat question." This question and the problems connected with it gave rise to a just social reaction and caused the impetuous emergence of a great burst of solidarity between workers, first and foremost industrial workers [*LE*, no. 8].

This reaction, which is described a little further on as an "ethically just social reaction," was elicited by the imposition of capitalism as "an economic and social system" (*LE*, no. 7). The reaction sprang from the real poverty and injustice created by an advancing industrialization that paid no heed to the human rights of workers.

The same complex set of historical relationships is also to be found in the majority of the peoples of Third World countries.

The present situation of the poor sectors and countries of the world has in large measure resulted from the predominance of the modern individualist spirit, which is alert to its own interests but myopic when it comes to the claims of others in both the social and the economic areas. At the opening of the Puebla Conference in Mexico, John Paul II spoke of the mechanisms "that lead on the international level to the ever-increasing wealth of the rich at the expense of the ever-increasing poverty of the poor" (Opening Address at Puebla, III, 4). He was pointing to a present situation that is the result of a historical process of universal scope. The issue is not simply economic and social; it is human. That is why *Laborem Exercens* speaks of an "ethical" reaction.

For the same reason — and this is of the first importance — the movement of liberation that proceeds from "the underside of history" is not purely and simply a continuation of the movement for modern freedoms. Far from it! The discontinuities and oppositions between the two have theoretical significance and therefore very extensive practical consequences. There are also, of course, threads of continuity between the two, as there always are in this kind of historical process. But if we do not see the discontinuities and contrasts, we will end up attributing both movements to the same impulse and classifying them under the same heading; in that case, we will lose sight of what is specific to each and become confused about the challenges to be met. *Libertatis Conscientia* does not appear to perceive this sufficiently.

The human and ethical level of which I have been speaking is the specific terrain of theological reflection that springs from the faith experience of the poor. Those with whom theologians dialogue here are those not looked upon and rated as persons in the present social order, those whose human dignity is systematically trampled down, those who are regarded as less important than the fruit of their work.

Those addressed in modern theology are different, and it is only right to take this fact into account. Modern theology is called upon to answer the questions raised by the modern consciousness and perceptively expressed by the Enlightenment. For if theology is done in the service of evangelization, then it must find the language needed for the Christian message to be effectively present in the modern world, the world in which the church, too, is living. Modern theology is therefore a necessary theology that has to meet the challenges of unbelievers and counteract the secularizing influence these challenges exert in the Christian world.

The theology being done in Latin America (and in other areas of the poor world) has a different point of departure. It is a reflection arising from "the underside of history," to which I referred earlier—that is, from the place where the historical results of the process carried through by the rich countries are to be seen. Theology is, of course, first of all an understanding illumined by faith, and its ultimate criteria of truth are derived from the "deposit of faith." But our thinking as human beings is always affected by the world in which we live and by the questions that world puts to us; this means that our theological thinking must relate to the faith as lived in and by the church in the historical phase through which it is passing.

Liberation theology, therefore, is not (as some think) the radical wing of European progressivist theology. The latter is facing challenges that are not ours, or at least are not primary for us. This point must be kept clearly in mind if there is to be any fruitful theological dialogue.[66] For there is a magnanimous tendency in some European circles to extend their internal debates to include theologies they persist in regarding as less scientific and less politically radicalized appendices to what is going on in the old continent![67]

I am obviously not claiming that, simply because we here are attempting to reflect within our own reality of poverty and within the life of our church, others must accept everything we do under pain of being otherwise considered bad Christians or oppressors. That would be inadmissible. What we do ask, in the name of openness to the Spirit that breathes where it will and in the name of respect for our people, is that others acknowledge the viewpoint we adopt and the questions we are trying to answer. Everything else must be an object of theological discussion and meet the requirements, which all must respect, of doctrinal orthodoxy and scientific work.

The Right of the Poor to Think. Theological discourse that is immersed in the life of the poor and accepts all the consequences this immersion entails cannot ignore the faith of the people.[68] The peoples of Latin America are both exploited and Christian. A failure to be attentive to both dimensions would mean a distortion of this complex reality; furthermore, each leaves its stamp on theological work.[69]

The modern world may think of itself as distant from God, but the same is not true in the world of the poor, where the question of God is a profound and decisive one. In sacred scripture contempt for the poor implies contempt for God; passages to this effect are beyond counting. It is not surprising, therefore, that the blindness of the modern mind to the poor, a blindness resulting from the economic and social order that mind inspires, should also find expression in distance from the God of Jesus Christ and the demands God makes of human beings.

Libertatis Conscientia criticizes modern individualism for its aloofness from God;[70] to this aloofness must be added its remoteness from the poor and their just demands. These are but two sides of the same coin, a fact that accounts for the constant criticism of the modern world (whose good points, however, are also recognized) in the kind of theological thinking done from the viewpoint of those whom James Cone calls "the victims of history." By the same token, and in a reversal of that historical development, sensitivity to the rights of the poor brings us closer to the God of life. "The spiritual . . . is not opposed to the social. The real opposition is between bourgeois individualism and the spiritual in the biblical sense."[71]

Liberation theology is anything but the Latin American spearhead of the secularizing thrust or of a "bourgeois Christianity." We think rather that a clear rejection, inspired by Christian faith, of the inhuman poverty existing in Latin America will militate against the negative side of secularism and the modern spirit. We are convinced that liberation thinking starts from a social, cultural, and religious situation differing from that of Europe and that this situation offers unparalleled historical possibilities that we must explore and develop. Not to do so would be an infidelity to the gospel and a betrayal of the poor of Latin America. Liberation thinking contributes to a sound and profound Christian identity that in turn makes possible a fruitful relationship with those Latin Americans who do not share the Christian faith but are committed to the poor and honestly sensitive to the Christian dimension in the life of the Latin American peoples.

The defense of life and the struggle for justice in Latin America bear the mark of faith in the God of life.[72] At the very beginning of the evangelization of Latin America Bartolomé de Las Casas preached a God who is alive amid the situation of death that was evident even then. The process of liberation has been watered by the blood of humble peasants and settlers who have endeavored to bear witness to their Christian faith through solidarity with their poorer brothers and sisters. The same is true of outstanding churchmen such as Bishops Enrique Angelelli and Oscar Romero, who, in addition, made clear their acceptance of this pastoral and theological perspective.

While the movement for the modern freedoms displayed aspects of distance from God and from the poor, the process of liberation that is now going on in Latin America is pregnant with new forms of closeness to the God of life and to the poor in their situation of death. Any effort to assimilate these two movements is not only historically inaccurate but, above all, would be a serious mistake in face of the demands laid upon us by our duty to bear witness and proclaim the reign of God.

There is no question of denying the ambivalence that marks every historical development; on the contrary, we must be attentive to them. But this ought not prevent us from being sensitive to their human and Christian possibilities. To thwart them out of fear that history may repeat itself would be to display too mean-spirited an analysis of the situation and a lack of hope in the God who makes all things new (see Rev. 21:5).

Libertatis Conscientia is accurate when it says that "a new phase in the history of freedom is opening before us" (no. 24). In this phase, interpretations of the past are as important as the possibilities and special features of the present.

CHRIST, THE LORD OF HISTORY

Integral liberation in Christ is the primary datum for thinking about the theme of liberation. The work of Christ is an efficacious call to full communion with the Father and for that reason has repercussions even now within history. Liberation is the way to freedom and beyond freedom to communion with God, to the Pauline "face to face." This it is that gives meaning and profound unity to a process in which it is possible and necessary to distinguish levels in order to understand better the free and unmerited gift of God's love.

Salvation and History

The central focus of the Lord's message is on the kingdom of God: a kingdom of life, love, truth, peace, justice, and freedom. "The kingdom is at hand," Jesus tells us at the beginning of his preaching (Mk. 1:15; Mt. 4:17). And, in a passage that John Paul II describes as "the first messianic program" (encyclical *Rich in Mercy*, no. 3), Luke specifies the content of Jesus' preaching: "The Spirit of the Lord is upon me, because he has anointed me to preach good news to the poor. He has sent me to proclaim release to the captives and recovery of sight to the blind, to set at liberty those who are oppressed, to proclaim the acceptable year of the Lord" (Lk. 4:18–19).[73]

Salvation in Christ gives human history as a whole its ultimate meaning and elevates it beyond itself. But for that very reason this salvation is already present in history; God's saving action is working upon history from within. History will be judged in terms of God's will as expressed in the kingdom.[74] The relation between kingdom and history is a major theme of theology, but my concern here is only with two points having to do with the integral character of liberation in Jesus Christ. The two points find expression in themes and passages of the Bible on the one hand and the magisterium on the other. These themes and passages help us grasp the deep unity of history, but the assertion of unity does not at all mean that we may not perceive and establish distinctions needed in order to avoid confusions and indeed even in order to assess properly the basic unity being affirmed.

An Experience of God as Liberator. Both *Libertatis Nuntius* and *Libertatis Conscientia* emphasize the part played by the exodus in our effort to grasp the meaning of liberation in the Bible.[75]

That saving event shows clearly the global scope of God's liberating action. "The major and fundamental event of the exodus . . . has a meaning that is both religious and political" (*LC*, no. 44). Both aspects are in fact present in the experience; the latter cannot, therefore, be reduced to only one of them.[76]

The one aspect does not negate the other; rather they are at different levels of depth. This is the important point to be kept in mind, for otherwise the message is mutilated. The ultimate meaning of the event is to be found in God's call to the people, inviting all of them to enter into full communion with God. This process takes place within a concrete history:

> Yahweh summons Israel not only to leave Egypt but also and above all to "bring them up out of that country into a fine, broad land; it is a land flowing with milk and honey" (3:8). The exodus is the long march toward the promised land in which Israel can establish a society free from misery and alienation. Throughout the whole process, the religious event is not set apart. It is placed in the context of the entire narrative, or, more precisely, it is its deepest meaning. It is the root of the situation. In the last instance, it is in this event that the dislocation introduced by sin is resolved and justice and injustice, oppression and liberation, are determined. Yahweh liberates the Jewish people politically in order to make them a holy nation: "You have seen with your own eyes what I did to Egypt. . . . If only you will now listen to me and keep my covenant, then out of all peoples you shall become my special possession; for the whole earth is mine. You shall be my kingdom of priests, my holy nation" (19:4-6). . . . The covenant gives full meaning to the liberation from Egypt; one makes no sense without the other.[77]

This is a point about which we must remain clear: priority belongs to the religious element, to the covenant with Yahweh, because it is this that gives the entire movement its deeper meaning. On the other hand—and this should be obvious—when we remind ourselves of the fact that the exodus of the Jewish people was also a social and political liberation, we are not thereby laying greater emphasis on this aspect than on the proper goal and ultimate meaning of the entire movement. The point of the reminder is rather to indicate the comprehensive character and broad scope of the covenant in the liberating event that was the exodus.[78]

It is because of this comprehensiveness that the event of the exodus can be called paradigmatic for biblical faith. The term "paradigm" is often used in the biblical sciences. The sense is not that the event must be repeated as such in the history of the Christian community but rather that the deeper meaning of the event — the liberating intervention of God — is permanently valid.

This presence of the Lord, together with his gift of full communion, gives unity to a process of liberation whose several aspects (and the differences between them) we may not overlook. From this point of view, the exodus truly plays an important part in liberation theology. Its importance should not be exaggerated, however, since other themes and other passages of the Bible also have a decisive role in this theological approach.[79]

More Human Conditions. There is a passage in the writings of Paul VI that played a decisive role in my approach to human history as a complex unity. The passage is no. 21 of the encyclical *Populorum Progressio,* and it deals with integral liberation. This passage helped me to establish the distinction between the three levels of a single process of liberation.[80]

Integral development is seen here as a passage from less human to more human living conditions. The pope says: "Less human conditions: the lack of material necessities for those who are without the minimum essential for life, the moral deficiencies of those who are mutilated by selfishness. Less human conditions: oppressive social structures, whether due to the abuses of ownership or to the abuses of power, to the exploitation of workers or to unjust transactions." The pope is speaking of an infrahuman situation that must be rejected in a movement toward more human conditions.

He goes on to say:

Conditions that are more human: the passage from misery toward the possession of necessities, victory over social scourges, the growth of knowledge, the acquisition of culture. Additional conditions that are more human: increased esteem for the dignity of others, the turning toward the spirit of poverty, cooperation for the common good, the will and desire for peace. Conditions that are still more human: the human acknowledgment of supreme values, and of God as their source and their finality.

The elimination of misery and the right to have the necessities of life are fundamental requirements for a human and just society. But this is not enough; other values must also be promoted: human dignity, the will for peace, ethical sensitivity, an openness to God.

"Conditions that, finally and above all, are more human: faith, a gift of God accepted by human good will, and unity in the charity of Christ, who calls us all to share as sons and daughters in the life of the living God, the Father of all." Here the process advances toward a human plenitude. The pope describes several things as "more human ... above all": faith, charity, and adoption as God's children, insofar as these divine gifts are freely accepted by human beings. This does not, of course, mean that God's gifts are being reduced to the purely human level. The pope is simply reminding us of an ancient Christian theme: complete human fulfillment comes only through elevation to the order of grace.

This important passage shows the different phases to be parts of a profound continuity and unity. Paul VI thus threw significant light on the problems that we were facing at that time in our pastoral activity.

The unified approach that liberation theology was beginning to take was confirmed by another important document of the magisterium. I am referring to the well-known passage in Medellín's document on justice: "It is the same God who in the fullness of time sent the Son in order that he might become flesh and save all human beings from *all the forms of enslavement* to which sin keeps them in subjection: ignorance, hunger, misery, and oppression, or, in short, the injustice and hatred that spring from human selfishness" (*Justice*, no. 3; italics added).

Liberation from sin by Christ (a central theme in liberation theology, as we shall see) attacks the ultimate root of all injustice and thus links together, though without confusing them, the several dimensions of liberation. In the passage just cited, the bishops gathered at Medellín were acknowledging the social significance of liberation in Christ: an aspect given little attention at that time. Clear reference is made to this same aspect in *Libertatis Conscientia*: "The work of salvation is thus seen to be indissolubly linked to the task of improving and raising the conditions of human life in this world" (no. 80).

The passages I have cited were and still are central for an understanding of salvation in human history. The Bible and the magisterium are at one in showing us a perspective, forestalling dangers, and, above all, reminding us how all-embracing is God's free and gratuitous will that the human race in its historical course should experience life.[81]

The Chalcedonian Principle

The idea that "there are three levels of meaning of a single, complex process, which finds its deepest sense and its full realization in the saving work of Christ" (*Liberation*, p. 25) is fundamental to my perspective and has its basis in a classic theological viewpoint, as Karl Lehmann acknowledges.[82] Also to be kept in mind is the fact that with this distinction (not separation) in mind, liberation theology was the first to speak of "total and integral liberation," a phrase much used nowadays. The passage from Paul VI on integral development, which I cited above, played a role here.

As I said, in order to avoid all kinds of confusion we must distinguish three levels of meaning in the liberation process. The three must then be conjoined, but as parts of "a single, complex process." The word "complex" is deliberately used in order to stress that we must avoid confusions and simplistic identifications.

The passage just cited (at note 30) goes on to say that "these levels of meaning . . . are interdependent"; that is, we are dealing with different things that are nonetheless connected with one another. At work here is the old Scholastic principle of which Jacques Maritain so perceptively reminded us all in recent decades: we must "distinguish in order to unite," and not in order to separate or confuse. "These three levels mutually affect each other, but they are not the same. One is not present without the others, but they are distinct: they are all part of a single, all-encompassing salvific process, but they are to be found at different levels."[83]

The complex unity comes, in the final analysis, from "Christ the savior," who "liberates from sin, which is the ultimate root of all disruption of friendship and of all injustice and oppression [first level]. Christ makes humankind truly free [second level] — that is to say, he enables us to live in communion with him; and this is the basis for all human fellowship [third level]" (*Liberation*, p. 25).

The stress, therefore, is on the third level: the work of Christ that liberates us from sin and brings us into communion with him. The changes that may take place in the social sphere are important, but they are also inadequate from the Christian viewpoint. For "a social transformation, no matter how radical it may be, does not automatically achieve the suppression of all evils."[84]

Distinguish in order to unite: but the issue is to achieve a unity that is not simply the sum of the parts but one that has a directing and ultimately decisive focal point. The theological approach here is inspired by the Council of Chalcedon, which defined that in Christ there are two natures, the human and the divine, which are distinct but neither confused nor separated. Furthermore, the profound unity given by the divine person in virtue of being the Son does not suppress the human nature of Christ. My treatment of "total or integral liberation" is inspired by this Chalcedonian principle.[85]

This idea of unity without confusion was also emphasized at Medellín. Here is a passage that clearly shows the mind of the Latin American bishops:

> While avoiding confusions or simplistic identifications, it [catechetical teaching] must always make clear the profound unity that exists between God's plan of salvation realized in Christ, and human aspirations; between the history of salvation and human history; between the

church, the people of God, and the temporal communities; between the revelation of God and human experience; between the supernatural gifts and charisms and human values [*Catechesis*, no. 4].

The unified approach arises from the conviction that the gratuitous gift of God's love is all-embracing. That which comes from God cannot affect only one sector of human life; that would be too narrow a conception of God's work. The challenge is to maintain the distinctions that allow us to understand the various levels of gratuitousness, while at the same time not separating human life into watertight compartments, as if there were areas of life into which the love of God, which is always free and unmerited, does not enter. *Libertatis Conscientia* says:

It is of course important to make a careful distinction between earthly progress and the growth of the kingdom, which do not belong to the same order. Nonetheless, this distinction is not a separation; for the human vocation to eternal life does not suppress but confirms the task of using human energies and means received from the creator for developing temporal life [no. 60].

The basic elements of the process are God's call and the free response of human beings: a response marked by the tenacity proper to the freedom that the Lord wants them to have.

The Peruvian bishops therefore make this carefully worded statement:

If by the history of salvation we mean not only properly divine actions — creation, incarnation, redemption — but also the actions of human beings insofar as these are responses, either positive or negative, to the initiatives of God, then there is really only one history, and the halting efforts of human beings become part of God's plans, whether they know it or not and whether they like it or not. Christ, God's Son made human, has given a perfect response, but all other human beings are called to share in it. There can be no denying the supernaturality and gratuitousness of the order of grace. What is needed, then, is to distinguish clearly without separating [*Documento*, no. 51].

The issue is here stated with all possible clarity; this is in fact the approach taken.

Contemporary Theology and the Unity of History

This unified view of history is not the private possession of liberation theology, but common in contemporary theology. Among other sources, it emerged from discussions on the relationship of grace to nature that went on in the first half of the present century among such theologians as Yves de Montcheuil, Henri de Lubac, Karl Rahner, Hans Urs von Balthasar, Juan Alfaro, and others.[86] The end result was unequivocal: a retrieval of the traditional approach (which St. Augustine so strongly emphasized), which says that in the concrete, human history is permeated at every point by the opposition between grace and sin. Juan Alfaro has shown that this was also St. Thomas' real position.[87] The distinctions his philosophical tools (Aristotelianism) enabled him to make with greater clarity (but which became inflexible in the later Scholasticism of Cajetan and others) did not alter this approach; they were simply that: needed distinctions.

Adopting this historical perspective, I wrote in *A Theology of Liberation*: "Historically and concretely we know humanity only as actually called to meet God" (*Liberation*, p. 45). The basic statement here is that from the viewpoint of faith "the history of salvation is the very heart of human history" (ibid., p. 86). Consequently, "the historical destiny of humanity must be placed definitively in the salvific horizon" (ibid., pp. 86–87). At issue here is the primacy of grace and of God's action in history.[88]

From this standpoint I have criticized the "distinction of planes model" (see *Liberation*, chap. 5), but this criticism by no means signifies a rejection of the distinction between nature and grace. What I challenge is a particular theology (one that is very fruitful in certain respects, as I pointed out a number of times in *A Theology of Liberation*) — namely, the "New Christendom" approach (see *Liberation,* chap. 4), which indeed supplies a clear scheme for dealing with the questions that are of concern to liberation theology (years ago, I myself adopted the "New Christendom" theological approach). What I reject—on theological grounds, not on grounds of faith—is "the existence of two juxtaposed 'orders,' closely connected or convergent," because the two are regarded as "deep down different from each other" (*Liberation,* p. 104).

The productive theological discussion of these themes that went on in the church made it possible to conclude that "in reality there is no pure nature and there never has been; there is no one who is not invited to communion with the Lord, no one who is not affected by grace."[89] The viewpoint adopted here is that of the concrete form taken by the economy of salvation. This viewpoint not only does not hinder, but it even necessarily demands the distinction between nature and grace for a proper understanding of this concrete unity. For this reason, *A Theology of Liberation* rejects any monolithic unity and speaks always of a "complex unity." For the same reason, it posits a distinction of levels, which is taken over from the "distinction of planes" model but lays greater stress on the concrete unity of the economy of salvation.[90]

As a matter of fact, all of this flows from a single, but fundamental, biblical datum: all things were created and have now been redeemed in Christ (a theme often found in St. John and St. Paul). At bottom, the unity comes from him, but the distinction between creation and redemption remains.[91]

The distinction is clearly shown in Ephesians 1:4: "He [God the Father] chose us in him [Christ] before the foundation of the world." The choice, or election, was to make us adoptive sons and daughters, and, contrary to the picture we sometimes draw for ourselves, it took place before creation. The "before" does not indicate a chronological precedence but a precedence of meaning and finality; we live in "a 'Christo-finalized' history."[92]

Let me repeat: Christ, who is both God and human, is the basis of a unity that does not do away with distinctions but does prevent confusions and separations. It is from this standpoint that theologians speak of creation as a "saving act."[93]

Within the basic affirmations required by the faith (nature and grace), theologians have continued to discuss this subject. The reason is that there are no perfect formulas in this area, and the theologians seek to develop those that will display a greater fidelity to the word of the Lord and the teachings of the church.

For this reason, after saying (in *A Theology of Liberation*) that "historically and concretely we know humanity only as actually called to meet God," I go on to add: "But an even more precise formulation has been sought in an effort to be faithful both to the gratuitous quality of God's gift as well as to its unified and all-embracing character" (*Liberation*, p. 45). The caution implicitly urged here is repeated a number of times; here is another passage:

> It seems, however, that contemporary theology has not yet fashioned the categories that would allow us to think through and express adequately this unified approach to history. We work, on the one hand, under the fear of falling back again into the old dualities, and, on the other, under the permanent suspicion of not sufficiently safeguarding divine gratuitousness or the unique dimension of Christianity [*Liberation*, p. 86].

The same concern led me to be more nuanced in my criticism of a dualist approach; at the end of it I referred to a passage in which Hans Urs von Balthasar points out, "ironically but perceptively" (ibid., p. 195, n. 44), the simplifications into which persons can fall when they reject every kind of distinction (ibid.). The truth is, we are dealing here with a theological question that is open to discussion and still not worked through completely.

The reader should be clear, then, that when I reject the existence of two histories, I am saying only that *in the actual order* of the economy of salvation there is not a history of nature and another history of grace, a history of fellowship and another of sonship and daughterhood. Rather, the connection between grace and nature, between God's call and the free response of human beings, is located within a single Christo-finalized history.

Libertatis Conscientia says pertinently that "the distinction between the supernatural order of salvation and the temporal order of human life must be seen in the context of God's singular plan to recapitulate all things in Christ" (no. 80).

FREEDOM AND COMMUNION

There is, then, a total liberation, the unity of which comes in the final analysis from communion with God and others, and in which three levels of meaning are distinguishable. This is a claim made in liberation theology from its very beginnings; it is often heard today when the subject is raised, whether in theological studies or in documents of the magisterium.[94]

This approach closely links liberation, freedom, and communion: three concepts to which I shall be referring in the following pages.

The freedom to which we are called presupposes the going out of oneself, the breaking down of our selfishness and of all the structures that support our selfishness; the foundation of this freedom is openness to others. The fullness of liberation — a free gift from Christ — is communion with God and with other human beings.

Summarizing what has been said above, we can distinguish three reciprocally interpenetrating levels of meaning of the term *liberation*, or, in other words, three approaches to the process of liberation [*Liberation*, p. 24].

At Puebla a similar formulation occurs at the beginning of a lengthy discussion of the three planes of liberation and their reciprocal relationships: "Freedom always implies the capacity we all possess in principle to be our own person and to act on our own initiative, so that we can go on fashioning community and participation to be embodied in definitive realities, on three inseparable planes: our relationship to the world as its master, to other persons as brothers or sisters, and to God as God's children" (no. 322).[95]

It is important to look at these levels or planes in detail, in order to get beneath the surface of each and to show how they imply one another within the controlling context of God's saving action.

Social Liberation

Medellín spoke very clearly of the situation of "dismal poverty, which in many cases becomes inhuman wretchedness" (*Poverty*, no. 1). It also said that the situation was not inevitable: "misery, as a collective fact, expresses itself as injustice that cries to the heavens" (*Justice*, no. 1); that is, it has causes for which human beings are responsible:

> In many instances Latin America finds itself faced with a situation of injustice that can be called institutionalized violence, when, because of a structural deficiency of industry and agriculture, of national and international economy, of cultural and political life, "whole towns lack necessities . . . ," thus violating fundamental rights. Such a situation demands global, daring, urgent, and profoundly renovative transformations [*Peace*, no. 16].[96]

Libertatis Conscientia echoes this denunciation of "institutionalized violence," which such polemics provoked and still provoke:

> In the systematic recourse to violence presented as the only way to liberation, it is necessary to denounce a destructive illusion, which leads to new servitudes. It must be condemned with the same vigor as the violence exercised by landowners against the poor, political outrages, and every form of *violence* set up as a form of government [no. 76, emphasis added].[97]

From this reality, "a deafening clamor breaks out, from millions of human beings, begging their pastors for a liberation that does not come to them from anywhere" (*Poverty*, no. 2). Some years later, Puebla states that this cry "may have seemed subdued at that time, but now it is clear, growing, impetuous, and, on occasion, threatening" (no. 89). "It is the cry of a people suffering, demanding justice, freedom, respect for fundamental personal and social rights" (no. 87).

These texts, among many others, set the terms for liberation at this level: an inhuman state of affairs, an unjust order—the principal cause of poverty—that must be changed, and a cry for liberation that comes from millions of the poor.[98] *Libertatis Conscientia* begins with a reference to these needed changes:

Awareness of human freedom and dignity, together with the affirmation of the inalienable rights of individuals and peoples, is one of the major characteristics of our time. But freedom demands conditions of an economic, social, political, and cultural kind, which make possible its full exercise. A clearer perception of the obstacles that hinder its development and offend human dignity is at the source of the powerful aspirations to liberation at work in our world [no. 1; see nos. 17 and 61].[99]

The Political Sphere. The passage from *Libertatis Conscientia* makes it clear that there is a situation here from which we may not turn away if we want to be faithful to the God of life, in solidarity with our brothers and sisters, especially the poor. For the sake of a better knowledge of this social reality and in the interests of commitment to those living in that situation, we may look to the social sciences for help.[100] (The problems and challenges entailed in this recourse to social analysis are dealt with in the article "Theology and the Social Sciences," reprinted in this volume.)

The field of society and politics is always tricky and challenging. It will be useful, therefore, to recall some points regarding it. Two meanings of "political" must be distinguished: a broader or more inclusive use, and a more specific one. In the broader use of the term, the political sphere "is the sphere for the exercise of a critical freedom won through history. It is the universal determinant and the collective arena for human fulfillment." The second use depends on the first: "Only within this broad meaning of the political sphere can we situate the more precise notion of 'politics' as an orientation to power. For Max Weber this orientation constitutes the typical characteristics of political activity."[101]

The first, inclusive meaning of the term "political" refers to the field in which "a person emerges as a free and responsible being, as a person in relationship with other persons, as someone who takes on a historical task" (*Liberation*, p. 31). The word "political" must therefore not be understood exclusively in its second meaning, which brings specific techniques into play and implies the choice of a party. Only the broad meaning allows us to say, for example, that in the historical life of a human being "nothing lies outside the political sphere *understood in this way*. Everything has a political color."[102]

Just as the political sphere is one dimension of human existence, so too liberation in that sphere is one level within an all-embracing process that takes its meaning from liberation from sin and communion with God and other human beings. Because sin is the breaking of friendship with God and neighbor, it is "the ultimate root" of all injustice (as the two Vatican Instructions put it). I shall return to this point; for the moment I wish only to repeat the perceptive and critical observation of G. Thils concerning *Libertatis Nuntius*: "If one sees sin as the 'ultimate root' of injustices and oppressions, one is also implicitly recognizing that all of these have more or less the same explanation."[103]

Social and political liberation aims at eliminating the proximate causes of poverty and injustice. This is required by the situation in which the vast majority of Latin Americans live. But let me repeat that "to affirm that all human reality has a political dimension in no way means, as the term itself indicates, to reduce everything to this dimension."[104] "Dimension," after all, is a term from spatial geometry; a body has three dimensions but is not reducible to one of them. The term is applied to human existence in order to bring out its complexity and richness; so too it is applied to the process of liberation.[105]

Social Conflict. The social conflict to be seen in the situation of poverty and misery is a fact acknowledged in *Libertatis Nuntius* (see VII, 8) and at various points in *Libertatis Conscientia*. The subject is a tricky one, and I have analyzed it in my article,

"Theology and the Social Sciences," in connection with one of its most difficult manifestations: confrontation between groups and social classes. Concerning this kind of confrontation I wish only to make it clear that I am far from regarding social conflict, and in particular the class struggle, as "an objective, necessary law" (*LN*, VIII, 7) or "the fundamental law of history" (IX, 2) or "the driving force of history" (IX, 3) or "an alleged law of history" (*LC*, no. 77). These formulas represent an attempt to elevate factual situations to the status of suprahistorical principles; they pass from changeable, complex realities to rigid, simplistic formulas and turn social analysis into philosophical theory.

Let me repeat here what I said on this point in the abovementioned article. After some reflections on Marx and on the fact of confrontation between social classes, I stated:

> Despite all this, Marxist thought does contain expressions that turn class struggle from a simple fact in "the driving force of history" and, in more philosophical versions, a "law of history.". . . My only concern here is to insist that this approach does not reflect my own thinking and therefore I have never used such expressions.[106]

Indeed, I am far from thinking of social conflict in that way.

Social liberation is necessary if any attempt is to be made to build a society based on respect for others, especially the weakest and least important. In other words, a society based not on the modern individualism of which I spoke in the first part of this essay but on a proper social understanding—a society in which the hunger for bread will disappear, as a deeply moved John Paul II said in his response to the words of the people of Villa San Salvador, during his visit to Peru.

These observations indicate one reason why I often speak of a "qualitatively different" society. It will be qualitatively different because other persons will be normative in a society in which the needs of the poor are more important than the power of the privileged—qualitatively different, too, because the goal will no longer be to incorporate more individuals into a consumer society but to change the way in which human beings are viewed.

But this takes us to the second level of liberation.

By way of conclusion to this section, let me say only that this necessary social liberation for which Medellín and Puebla call and which liberation theology emphasizes does not exhaust the human aspiration for liberation. A change at this level is important but not sufficient; more than that, it would be ambiguous, especially if not followed by other, deeper changes. My grasp of this point led me, twenty years back, to say very clearly: "Christian hope opens us, in an attitude of spiritual childhood, to the gift of the future promised by God. It keeps us from any confusion of the kingdom with any one historical stage, from any idolatry toward unavoidably ambiguous human achievement, from any absolutizing of revolution" (*Liberation*, p. 139).

The Freedom of the Human Person

A radical change of the socio-economic order that creates poverty in Latin America is something we must demand as human beings and as Christians. The criteria we apply in making judgments must not stop short at isolated facts but must "concern economic, social, and political systems" (*LC*, no. 74). This will to make changes is based on a conviction that social structures do not arise from "an alleged determinism of history" but "depend on the responsibility of humankind, who can alter them" (ibid.).

The need and the conviction bring me to what I have been calling the second dimension of liberation, a dimension in which human freedom plays a key role. We are now at a deeper level, involving "an understanding of history. Humankind is seen as assuming conscious responsibility for its own destiny. This understanding provides a dynamic context and broadens the horizons of the desired social changes. In this perspective the unfolding of all the dimensions of humanness is demanded — persons who make themselves throughout their life and throughout history."[107]

While the social dimension is of the utmost importance, it is only one side of liberation. Awareness of the different human possibilities and the assumption of historical responsibility are one manifestation of what Vatican II called "a new humanism"; "We are witnessing ... the birth of a new humanism, where humankind is defined before all else by responsibility to one's fellow human beings and at the court of history" (*Gaudium et Spes*, no. 55; Flannery, pp. 959-60).

Implicit here is the idea of the "new human being," an expression current in political philosophy and historical approaches to the problem, and intended to stress the point that new social structures are not enough. For structures always depend on concrete persons, and the latter must be involved if we want real change. This is true for every type of society, for society must be based not only on justice but also on freedom. That is why I wrote: "These personal aspects—considered not as excessively privatized, but rather as encompassing all human dimensions—are also under consideration in the contemporary debate concerning greater participation of all in political activity. This is so even in a socialist society."[108] The requirement is a universal one that knows no exceptions.

A change of social structures can help to bring about this personal change but does not automatically bring it about. On the other hand, there are also alleged transformations of persons that have no consequences in the social sphere. We must avoid falling victim to facile generalizations that do not adequately respect the autonomy proper to each level: "It is no more 'mechanistic' to think that a structure change automatically makes for a new humanity, than to think that a 'personal' change guarantees social transformations. Both assumptions are unreal and naive."[109]

In the approach I am taking, there is no room for a historical analysis based on economic determinism; the very assertion of freedom in all dimensions of the human already rejects this kind of determinism that impoverishes human history.[110] Structural change is necessary, but it is not everything. Human freedom has an interior dimension that is sometimes neglected due to the urgent demands of the commitment to justice. But, to offset that tendency, it is important to bear in mind that "modern human aspirations include not only liberation from *exterior* pressures, which prevent fulfillment as a member of a certain social class, country, or society. Persons seek likewise an *interior* liberation, in an individual and intimate dimension; they seek liberation not only on a social plane but also on a psychological plane"(*Liberation*, p. 20). This outlook is inconsistent with one that does not take the interior freedom of human beings into account, for this interior freedom is also the object of a powerful human aspiration. It remains true, therefore, that "for many persons in various ways this aspiration—in Vietnam or Brazil, New York or Prague—has become a norm for their behavior and a sufficient reason to lead lives of dedication."[111]

In my view, a society that is mindful of this interior liberation and the different dimensions of the human can likewise be called "qualitatively different." It is with this in mind that I have spoken on some occasions of "a social appropriation . . . of freedom" (*Liberation*, p. 139). My intention in using this expression is to distance myself from the individualist viewpoint which is one of the characteristics of the modern world and which many propose as a model for Latin America. I use it also in order to bring out the need of freedom for all. As was said during the discussions on religious freedom, freedom is indivisible. It is not possible to defend freedom for some and to deny it in practice to the majority. But this is what happens in even the best democratic phases in the life of our countries. Personal freedom must extend to the whole of society. Nor is the issue to secure freedom for *the majority*; no, the need is to ensure the freedom of all. This is the challenge we face in Latin America in the present process of liberation.

All that has been said makes it clear that the second level of liberation, which postulates the necessity of constructing a new human being, is located in history and requires human effort. The meaning of "new human being" here is not the meaning St. Paul gives the term when he opposes the new person or self to the old. The new human being of which St. Paul speaks is produced by the forgiveness of sin and the unmerited gift that makes men and women God's adoptive children. That is still another level of liberation in Christ, and it is the most decisive level. If I mention Paul here, it is because he "continuously reminds us . . . of the paschal core of Christian existence and of all of human life; the passage from the old to the new person, from sin to grace, from slavery to freedom. 'For freedom Christ has set us free' (Gal. 5:1), St. Paul tells us. He refers here to liberation from sin insofar as it represents a selfish turning in upon oneself" (*Liberation*, p. 23). But that, as I said, points us toward the third level of liberation.[112]

Let me end this section by saying that at this level are located the plans for a new society, the utopias that spur action in history. In this sense it can be said that "political liberation appears as the path toward the utopia of a freer, more human humankind, the protagonist of its own history" (*Liberation*, p. 38). At the same time, however, the journey must be made with respect for personal freedom, for this is not only the goal of the journey but the necessary condition for any authentic political liberation. *Libertatis Conscientia* reminds us of this: "A process of liberation that has been achieved can only create better conditions for the effective exercise of freedom. Indeed a liberation that does not take into account the personal freedom of those who fight for it is condemned to defeat in advance" (no. 31; see no. 26).

But for the very reason that this dimension of liberation is not restricted to what is usually understood by "the political sphere,"[113] it enables us to connect political liberation with liberation from sin, without either identifying or juxtaposing the two.[114]

Toward Full Communion

Both *Libertatis Nuntius* and *Libertatis Conscientia* firmly assert that the saving work of Christ is primarily a deliverance from sin, which is "the most radical form of slavery" (*LN*, IV, 2), "the most radical evil" (*LC*, no. 3), and the source of other slaveries and other evils.[115] The saving work of Christ is primarily what *Libertatis Conscientia* calls a "soteriological liberation."

As everyone knows, liberation from sin is a dominant theme in liberation theology and in my own contribution to it. I say this in all simplicity but also with conviction and clarity. In the treatment of some other themes, readers may find that one or another statement of liberation is unclear or needs to be put more carefully, but on this point there can be no doubt.[116] Because sin is a breaking of friendship with God and others, it is the ultimate root of all injustice and all division among human beings; God's grace alone can overcome sin.

We have here reached the third level of liberation and can see what gives it its radicality and makes it so all-embracing. "In the Bible, Christ is presented as the one who brings us liberation. Christ the Savior liberates from sin, which is the ultimate root of all disruption of friendship and of all injustice and oppression. Christ makes humankind truly free, that is to say, he enables us to live in communion with him; and this is the basis for all human fellowship."[117] It is the grace of Christ that liberates us from sin and enables us to live in communion. Let us look at these two points.

The Concept of Sin. Sin is a rejection of the gift of God's love. The rejection is a personal, free act. It is a refusal to accept God as Father and to love others as the Lord loves us. Only the action of God can heal human beings at the root of the self-centeredness that prevents them from going out of themselves.

There was a period (not that of the fathers of the church nor of the great medieval theologians) when the predominate type of theology neglected the social dimension of sin. In recent decades a growing awareness of the social problem has brought a return to the true perspective with its profound biblical roots; in addition, Medellín brought it to mind when it spoke of "a sinful situation" (*Peace*, no. 1).

Some were disturbed by this. But just before the Puebla Conference the pope summed up current thinking on this point and insisted on using, for example, the expression "sinful structure" (homily at the shrine of Zapopan). As a result, the theme received special emphasis at Puebla (see nos. 28, 70, 73, 92, 185, 186, 281, 452, 487, 515).[118] *Libertatis Conscientia*, for its part, observes: "In the light of the gospel, many laws and structures seem to bear the mark of sin and prolong its oppressive influence in society" (no. 54).

This is the setting for what liberation theology has to say on the subject. The emphasis on the social dimension of sin is due to the fact that this dimension was so little present to the Christian conscience at that time.[119] But the emphasis is thus placed chiefly because this perspective, based on the faith, enables us to understand better what has happened and is still happening in Latin America. This also accounts for the presence of the theme at Medellín and Puebla. The concern is fundamentally pastoral: "Faced with the situation of sin, the church has a duty to engage in denunciation. Such denunciation must be objective, courageous, and evangelical. Rather than condemning, it seeks to save both the guilty party and the victim" (Puebla, no. 1296).

This emphasis, however, by no means signifies a forgetfulness of the personal dimension of sin. The breaking of friendship with God is the action of a free will. Moreover, "behind an unjust structure there is a personal or collective will responsible—a willingness to reject God and neighbor" (*Liberation*, p. 24). Again, "because sin is a personal and social intrahistorical reality, a part of the daily events of human life, it is also, and above all, an obstacle to life's reaching the fullness we call salvation" (ibid., p. 85). Or, looking at it from a different angle, "sin is regarded as a social, historical fact, the absence of fellowship and love in relationships among persons, a breach of friendship with God and with other persons, and therefore, an interior, personal fracture" (ibid., p. 102).

As these passages show, the importance of the social consequences of sin does not mean forgetting that sin is always the result of a personal, free act. Thus *Libertatis Conscientia* says that "the sin at the root of unjust situations is, in a true and immediate sense, a voluntary act that has its source in the freedom of individuals. Only in a derived and secondary sense is it applicable to structures, and only in this sense can one speak of 'social sin'" (no. 75).[120] "Derived," because the reference is to the consequences of acts for which some person is responsible. Society as such does not perform free acts (these are the prerogative of persons), but it is affected by what flows from sin, as the texts I have cited show.[121]

John Paul II writes, therefore:

> To speak of *social* sin means in the first place to recognize that, by virtue of a human solidarity that is as mysterious and intangible as it is real and concrete, each individual's sin in some way affects others. . . . Consequently, one can speak of a *communion of sin*. . . . In other words, there is no sin, not even the most intimate and secret one, the most strictly individual one, that exclusively concerns the person committing it. With greater or lesser violence, every sin

has repercussions on the entire ecclesial body and the whole human family.[122]

In my own approach to theology, sin occupies a central place.[123] This breaking of friendship with God and others is a rejection of that "communion with the Lord and with all humans [which] is more than anything else a gift" (*Liberation*, p. 118). For this reason, "to sin is to refuse to love, to reject communion and fellowship, to reject even now the very meaning of human existence" (ibid., p. 113).

F. Moreno has brought out the christological perspective in which sin is treated in liberation theology. Here is what he says of sin's role in this theology: "If Latin American theology has given a privileged place to the discussion of sin, it is out of theological honesty and in order to reflect a situation in which real sin cries to heaven; it is also due to the consistency and adaptability of a theological method that is especially sensitive to and capable of capturing this dimension of reality" (Moreno, n. 117, p. 137).

Collaboration in the building of a just society is an act of solidarity and love; it demands resistance to that which is a negation of love: sin. But it is also clear that because sin is radical evil, it can be conquered only by the grace of God and the radical liberation that the Lord bestows. This grace of God is present in every act of authentic human love. The relationship between grace and sin is played out in the inmost depths of the human person.

Communion in Love. Liberation from sin is one side of the coin; the other is communion with God and others. According to a classic distinction, *freedom from* is directed toward *freedom for*.[124] It is to this *freedom for* that Christ's saving work is also directed. By nailing sin to the cross, Jesus opened the way for us to full communion with the Father. This communion discloses the meaning of our lives:

The knowledge that at the root of our personal and community existence lies the gift of the self-communication of God, the grace of God's friendship, fills our life with gratitude. It allows us to see our encounters with others, our loves, everything that happens in our life, as a gift. There is a real love only when there is free giving—without conditions or coercion. Only gratuitous love goes to our very roots and elicits true love [*Liberation*, p. 119].

The entire process of liberation is directed toward communion. Some pages back, I stated my agreement (a long-standing agreement, in fact) with an important theme in *Libertatis Conscientia*—that liberation is a way to freedom. But we must go further, for freedom is not an end in itself, but must be ordered to love and service.[125] In Galatians 5:1 Paul reminds us that Christ has set us free for freedom; and in 5:13 he speaks of true freedom as exercised in the form of love (cf. *Liberation*, 24). In the final analysis, freedom shows itself as openness to God and others. Although *Libertatis Conscientia* has some passages along this line,[126] it does not have any full development of the idea of communion as the ultimate purpose of liberation; it would have been helped here, had it approached the matter from the viewpoint of the Bible.[127]

The question that arises at this point is the connection between this grace of communion (and liberation from sin) and the first two levels of liberation. Puebla found an excellent formulation of the connection:

Authentic communion and participation can exist in this life only if they are projected on to the very concrete plane of temporal realities, so that mastery, use, and transformation of the goods of this earth and those of culture, science, and technology find embodiment in humanity's just and fraternal lordship over the world—which would include respect for ecology. Confronted with the realities that are part of our lives today, we must learn from the gospel that in Latin America we cannot truly love our fellow human beings, and hence God, unless we commit ourselves on the personal level, and in many cases on the structural level as well, to serving and promoting the most dispossessed and downtrodden human groups and social classes, with all the consequences that will entail on the plane of temporal realities (no. 327).

What we have here is not simply a theological formulation. This teaching of the magisterium proved to be a call that, together with the teaching of Medellín, inspired the activity, life, and death of many Latin American Christians: men and women who dared to live their communion with God in solidarity with the poor, the least of our society, and who accepted "all the consequences" that that solidarity entailed.

To distinguish these levels, which are located at different degrees of depth (*Liberation*, p. 103), is not to separate them. There is no question of "three parallel or chronologically successive processes. ... There are three levels of meaning of a single, complex process, which finds its deepest sense and its full realization in the saving work of Christ" (ibid., p. 25). This saving work is what gives the whole process its meaning:

> These levels of meaning, therefore, are interdependent. A comprehensive view of the matter presupposes that all three aspects can be considered together. In this way two pitfalls will be avoided: first, *idealist* or *spiritualist* approaches, which are nothing but ways of evading a harsh and demanding reality, and second, shallow analyses and programs of short-term effect initiated under the pretext of meeting immediate needs.[128]

The grace of God is a gift, but it also sets a task. The process by which we are saved includes both the gratuitous initiative of God and the free response of human beings. Our acceptance of the gift of adoptive filiation must find expression in the building of authentic brotherhood and sisterhood in history. Nothing is more demanding than gratuitousness, nothing calls for greater commitment. The elderly Paul tells Philemon that he expects him to "do even more than I say" (v. 21). Thereby he opens the door to the possibility of limitless work on Philemon's part in the service of his brother, who, in this case, is a man who is not acknowledged to be a human being with all human rights.[129]

Christians must in one or other fashion daily "invent" their life of love and commitment.

THE LIBERATING MISSION OF THE CHURCH

The truth that sets human beings free is Jesus himself: this perspective presided over the consideration set down in the first two parts of this essay. The task imposed on those whom he sets free (see Jn. 8:36) is to proclaim the saving truth that he came to bring us. The salvation in question I have been calling integral liberation, because, with liberation from sin as its starting point, it extends to all dimensions of the human.

The mission of the church, as the community of Jesus' disciples, is to communicate and bear witness to this total liberation of the human being. The liberation has, indeed, aspects that have a degree of autonomy (social liberation, liberation of the human person), but these are not watertight compartments into which the saving grace of Christ does not reach. The church must respect the inner coherence proper to each of these several areas; it does not have a right to give directives in fields that are the proper objects of human efforts. On the other hand, it does have a duty to show the connection of these areas with the kingdom of God and its ethical demands.

Furthermore, the church must remind human beings of the ultimate meaning and destiny of every human work. For, as a profound passage in *Gaudium et Spes* of Vatican II says:

> When we have spread on earth the fruits of our nature and our enterprise — human dignity, brotherly communion, and freedom — according to the command of the Lord and in his Spirit, we will find them once again, cleansed this time from the stain of sin, illuminated and transfigured, when Christ presents to his Father an eternal and universal kingdom "of truth and life, a kingdom of holiness and grace, a kingdom of justice, love, and peace." Here on earth the kingdom is mysteriously present; when the Lord comes it will enter into its perfection [no. 389; Flannery, p. 938].

At stake here is the very identity of the church and of its being and activity. The dialogue with the world presupposes that the church is aware of its difference from the world, not in order to distance itself from the world but precisely in order that it may be truly close to the world. For the church, of him who came to set up his tent in our midst (see Jn. 1:14), consciousness of its identity does not mean a defensive turning in upon itself. Neither does it mean that the church is not to be humbly but resolutely conscious of having a message that must be transmitted; it does not mean that the church is to be dissolved into the movement of history under pretext of serving that movement.

It is not an easy task to find the appropriate and fruitful way of manifesting this identity; but this is one of the most important demands made of the church at the present time. It is also the best way of showing fidelity to the Second Vatican Council, which laid special emphasis on the mystery of the church and its mission. Romano Guardini spoke of our age as "the time of the church"; the prophecy will be fulfilled to the extent that the church seeks "first the kingdom of God and its righteousness," because then everything else will be its as well (Mt. 6:33).

EVANGELIZING LIBERATION

"The Church's essential mission, following that of Christ, is a mission of evangelization and salvation. It draws its zeal from the divine love. Evangelization is the proclamation of salvation, which is a gift of God" (*LC*, no. 63). Due to the pastoral experiences and theological reflections that I have been presenting, this task of the church has in recent times been increasingly referred to as one of "liberating evangelization." In this regard, the episcopal conference at Medellín and the theology being done in Latin America have been an important influence. The apostolic exhortation *Evangelii Nuntiandi* then established the terms in which the evangelizing task of the church was to be described, and Puebla repeated *Evangelii Nuntiandi* in the Latin American context.[130] *Libertatis Conscientia* continues on the same line when it gives the title "The Liberating Mission of the Church" to its fourth chapter.

The church's mission is, as I said, to proclaim an integral

liberation, because nothing is left untouched by the saving work of Christ:

> The love that impels the church to communicate to all persons a sharing in the grace of divine life also causes it, through the effective action of its members, to pursue the true temporal good of persons, help them in their needs, provide for their education, and promote an integral liberation from everything that hinders the development of individuals. The church desires the good of humankind in all its dimensions [*LC*, no. 63].

Of these different dimensions we have treated previously. Proclamation of the message springs from contemplative experience that is characterized by joy in the Lord's gift:

> To know that the Lord loves us, to accept the free gift of his love, is the deep source of the joy and gladness of a person who lives by the word of God. *Evangelization is the communication of this joy.* It is the communication of the good news of the love of God that has changed our life. It is a free, gratuitous proclamation, just as the love in which it originates is free and gratuitous. In the point of departure of the task of evangelization, then, there is always an experience of the Lord—a living experience of the Father's love, the love that makes us God's daughters and sons, the love that transforms us, making us more fully human, more fully brothers and sisters to all [*Power*; italics added].

The joy that the love of God produces in us should characterize our proclamation of the divine will that we be set free.

At the same time, to proclaim the gospel is to call human beings together as a church: "To proclaim the gospel is to announce the mystery of filiation and fellowship . . . 'a mystery hidden for generations and centuries and . . . revealed' in Christ. Hence to proclaim the gospel is to summon persons together, summon them into *ekklesia*, into church" (*Power*, p. 67).

Kingdom and History

The Second Vatican Council chose the church as the focal point of its thinking.[131] In doing so, it made its own a decades-long effort to think through the mystery of the church, its role in the contemporary world, the relationship between the different Christian confessions, and the attitude to be adopted toward other religions. Vatican II refused to offer a definition of the church and sought rather to enter into the mystery of the church.[132] The category of "sacrament" seemed appropriate for this purpose, for it made it possible to bring together many aspects of the reality that is the church.

The idea of "sacrament" implies the idea of "sign," but the sign in this case is an efficacious sign. When the church is called "the universal sacrament of salvation" (*Lumen Gentium*, no. 48; Flannery, p. 407), what is meant is that it transforms the life of human beings. The power of the Spirit is present in the church:

> In the sacrament the salvific plan is fulfilled and revealed; that is, it is made present among humans and for humans. But at the same time, it is through the sacrament that humans encounter God. This is an encounter *in* history, not because God comes *from* history, but because history comes from God. The sacrament is thus the efficacious revelation of the call to communion with God and to the unity of all humankind [*Liberation*, p. 146].

The church is the sacrament of God's saving plan—that is, of the kingdom. It mediates an encounter inasmuch as God comes forth in search of human beings; the initiative belongs to God who, as we saw earlier, is not reducible to human history but is revealed in it. The revelation that the sacrament gives is efficacious and creative—provided human freedom consents—of communion with God and the unity of the human race. The church is the sacrament of this communion and unity (see *Lumen Gentium*, no. 1).

The nature or being of the church is the basis of its evangelizing activity. "The church can be understood only in relation to the reality that it announces to humankind. Its existence is not 'for itself,' but rather 'for others.' Its center is outside itself, it is in the work of Christ and his Spirit" (*Liberation*, p. 147). The power of the Spirit who "will guide you into all the truth" (Jn. 16:13) is the driving force in the church's evangelizing mission.

The church proclaims a plenitude and a life that will not be fully realized except beyond history, but that already affect the progress of humanity. The necessity of attending to the life of persons living today, in the context of a proclamation that looks beyond history, compels *Libertatis Conscientia* to say:

> When the church speaks about the promotion of justice in human societies or when it urges the faithful laity to work in this sphere according to their own vocation, it is not going beyond its mission. It is, however, concerned that this mission not be absorbed by preoccupations concerning the temporal order or reduced to such preoccupations. Hence it takes great care to maintain clearly and firmly both the unity and the distinction between evangelization and human promotion: unity, because it seeks the good of the whole person; distinction, because these two tasks enter in different ways into its mission [no. 64].

This matter must be looked at in the light of what I said earlier about the connection between the several levels of liberation. There must be both unity and distinction, as the passage just cited says. At the beginning of my work on liberation theology I said, at the end of a lengthy section devoted to this point: "Not only is the growth of the kingdom not reduced to temporal progress; because of the word accepted in faith, we see that the fundamental obstacle to the kingdom, which is sin, is also the root of all misery and injustice; we see that the very meaning of the growth of the kingdom is also the ultimate precondition for a just society and a new humanity" (*Liberation*, p. 103).

I went on to explain:

> This is not an identification. Without liberating historical events, there would be no growth of the kingdom. But the process of liberation will not have conquered the very roots of human oppression and exploitation without the coming

of the kingdom, which is above all a gift. Moreover, we can say that the historical, political liberating event *is* the growth of the kingdom and *is* a salvific event; but it is not *the* coming of the kingdom, not *all* of salvation. It is the historical realization of the kingdom and, therefore, it also proclaims its fullness [ibid., p. 104].

"Complete communion" is the controlling goal of the entire process (ibid.), and this communion is first and foremost a gift, a grace from the Lord. In this communion human beings reach their full liberation. For Christians, "the cross and the resurrection are the seal of our liberty" (ibid., p. 172).

The faith does not permit a reduction of the kingdom to any historical embodiment, however human and just we think it to be. We are in a different order of things here. This point is at the heart of the Christian message.[133] The fundamental statements in this area are clear, but the concrete ways of expressing the connection between the Christian message and human liberation are always a quarry, as it were, in which theologians must carve anew.

A few years back, Yves Congar asked himself what the connection is between "Christian salvation and the irrepressible movement for human liberations,"[134] and he suggested an interesting approach. After surveying the theme of the church as sacrament of salvation, he turned to another major idea of the council—one with an ancient biblical and patristic lineage—in order to make the question more specific. The church, which is the sacrament of salvation, is (Congar said) the people of God, the messianic people, in its totality; it is not simply the institution, though that is what the word "sacrament" might suggest to some.[135]

This identification gives a historical dynamism to the expression "universal sacrament of salvation," while at the same time the messianic character of this people refers us to Christ the messiah and to the way in which he conceived his task in regard to human liberations.

The eschatological justice that Christ proclaims inspires a critique of "situations and actions that God's plan for the human person condemns"; at the same time, it seeks "translation into human forms," which, however, it leaves "on their proper level and in their proper order." These considerations make it possible, says Congar, to raise the question of "faith and the political order," without succumbing to confusions. He concludes: "Always the Chalcedonian rule: no separation, no confusion" (this is the final sentence of his book).[136]

At an earlier point, he had said: "What is the sacrament of salvation? The people of God. Where and how? In all its life, in all its history, which it lives within the history of the world. This is why God [the Lord Jesus] has given us the Holy Spirit who spoke through the prophets."[137] The idea of the historical journey that the church makes as the sacrament that is identical with the people of God seems to me especially fruitful in connection with the subject I am treating here.

The mission of the Holy Spirit, which Congar emphasizes, is the central theme of a book of Jürgen Moltmann. I am interested here only in what relates to the question with which I am concerned at the moment. The German theologian regards as important but inadequate the christological foundation that both Barth and Rahner give to the idea of sacrament (he thinks their approaches are convergent, even though they start from different premises). In fact, the sacramentality of the church has been seen primarily in relation to Christ as the primordial sacrament. Adopting an ecumenical perspective, Moltmann goes so far as to ask: "Granted the remaining difference in the Protestant-Catholic convergence ... could this not be overcome through the trinitarian understanding of the eschatological gift of the Holy Spirit as the sacrament?"

To this end he calls upon the idea of mystery (*sacramentum*) as the revelation of God in history (an idea to which I referred earlier) and says that this can be understood only in an eschatological perspective. Thus viewed, "the use of the word 'mystery' spreads beyond christology and flows into pneumatology, ecclesiology, and the eschatology of world history."

The conclusion is inescapable and pregnant with consequences: "the sending of the Holy Spirit" is "the sacrament of the kingdom" and leads "the church beyond its own present existence into the world and drives it toward the perfected kingdom of God."[138] This foundation makes possible a better understanding of the role the church must play, on its historical journey, as it confronts whatever is out of harmony with the values of the kingdom.

These varying approaches show that thinking on these topics continues to be intense. Within the framework of the basic affirmations of faith on these topics, we must consider how the approaches look when seen in the Latin American context. Controlling principles in making our judgment must be our fidelity to the word of God and our rejection of all the forms of oppression under which the peoples of Latin America are suffering. As John Paul II said in his address to the episcopal conference at Puebla: "It is . . . not out of opportunism or a thirst for novelty that the church, the 'expert in humanity' (Paul VI, Address to the United Nations, October 5, 1965) defends human rights. It is prompted by an authentically evangelical commitment, which, like that of Christ, is primarily a commitment to those most in need" (III, 3).[139]

Evaluating what had been accomplished in Latin America, Puebla was therefore able to say:

> We are pleased to note many examples of efforts made to live out liberative evangelization in all its fullness. One of the chief tasks involved in continuing to encourage Christian liberation is the creative search for approaches free of ambiguity and reductionism (*Evangelii Nuntiandi*, no. 32) and fully faithful to the word of God. Given to us in the church, that word stirs us to offer a joyful proclamation to the poor as one of the messianic signs of Christ's kingdom [no. 488].

The proclamation of the good news to the poor is a sign of the presence of Christ the messiah in human history.[140]

The Mystery of Evangelization

Medellín said that the church must be "poor, *missionary*, and paschal."[141] The missionary perspective was very much present in Vatican II; it can even be said to have been the major inspiration of its documents. The council was concerned that the church move outside itself in service to the world and, in the final analysis, to the Lord of history, as *Gaudium et Spes* says.

This missionary inspiration is well expressed in *Ad Gentes*, which is one of the most richly theological documents of the council. In it mission is presented, in light of its trinitarian foundation, not as one among many activities of the church, but as a main trait of the Christian community as a whole. Medellín adopts the same perspective, but in terms of a church that has hitherto existed in a situation that might be described as "Christendom."

Puebla repeats the call to mission that was uttered at Medellín and speaks of "a missionary church that joyously proclaims to persons today that they are children of God in Christ; that commits itself to the liberation of the whole human being and all human beings . . . and that in solidarity immerses itself in the apostolic activity of the universal church" (no. 1304).

I should like to emphasize two things that have been characteristic of the Latin American church in this area.

The Poor Have the Gospel Preached to Them. Vatican II referred to this profound and demanding theme of the gospel, and Medellín made it central in its own reflections. There it supplied the context for the preferential option for the poor that inspired the principal documents of that conference and that has characterized the life of the Latin American church in the years since then. Many experiments have been undertaken and many commitments made in an effort to proclaim the message to the most disinherited. In proceeding along this line, the church has found itself in tune with the deep longing the poor of Latin America have for liberation.

All this has brought with it an extensive renewal in the church's way of acting. The call to mission always entails a going out of its own world and an entering into a different world. This is what sizable sectors of the Latin American church have experienced as they have embarked upon the evangelization of the poor and the oppressed: they have begun to discover *the world of the poor* (see *Drink*, pp. 124–26). That world is far more alien to the church than churchmen have been accustomed to think. It is a world that has deficiencies and limitations but also potentialities and riches. To be poor is to survive rather than live;[142]

it is to be subject to exploitation and injustice; it is also, however, to possess a special way of feeling, thinking, loving, believing, suffering, and praying. The proclamation of the gospel to the poor requires entering their world of wretchedness—and of hope.

The church in Latin America has only entered upon this road. It has made a beginning, however, of what is one form of openness to the world as called for by the council; in this case, openness to the world of poverty. The commitment has not been without its defects; nonetheless there is a definite will to solidarity with the real poor: "Those who are oppressed by poverty are the object of a love of preference on the part of the church, which ever since its origin and in spite of the failings of many of its members, has not ceased to work for their relief, defense, and liberation" (*LC*, no. 68).

This is not the first passage in which the 1986 Instruction acknowledges these failures in the historical course taken by the Christian community; the acknowledgment only enhances its emphasis on what ought to be, and in fact is, the mission of the church. Part of this mission is to meet the immediate needs of the poor, while at the same time promoting "structural changes in society so as to secure conditions of life worthy of the human person" (ibid.).

The efforts made are only beginnings, but they are real, and the other churches of Latin America can repeat what the church of Peru said recently in light of its own experience:

This message of liberation has in recent years inspired the life of the church in Peru, as it has numerous statements of the bishops, for it is a source of deeper spirituality. The church has achieved an important presence, as sign of hope and salvation, in society as a whole, and especially among the poorest and most marginalized [*Documento*, no. 10].

But this closeness to the poor also brings new challenges to which no response is possible apart from a deepening Christian maturity in the Spirit.

The Evangelizing Potential of the Poor. Puebla, like Medellín, emphasized the importance for the church of evangelizing the poor; this is a basic and abiding requirement of the gospel. At the same time, however, the years that had elapsed between the two conferences had made it possible to study the call to evangelization more thoroughly and discover new aspects of it.

They had been years of commitment "to defend the rights of the poor and oppressed according to the gospel commandment" (Medellín, *Peace*, no. 22); years, too, in which basic ecclesial communities were established as "the first and fundamental ecclesiastical nucleus, which . . . must make itself responsible for the richness and expansion of the faith" (Medellín, *Joint Pastoral Planning*, no. 10). These ecclesial experiences "have helped the church to discover the evangelizing potential of the poor" (Puebla, no. 1147).

The poor, the privileged (though not exclusive, as the document does say) addressees of the message of the kingdom, are also its bearers. One way in which they carry out this role is through the basic ecclesial communities that Puebla hails as one of the most important developments in the life of the Latin American church and as an embodiment of "the church's preferential love for the common people" (no. 643). In these communities, moreover, the poor "are given a concrete opportunity to share in the task of the church and to work with commitment for the transformation of the world" (ibid.).

One of the most interesting statements in *Libertatis Conscientia* is undoubtedly the one referring to this very important aspect of the church's life in Latin America:

> The new basic communities or other groups of Christians that have arisen to be witnesses to this evangelical love are a source of great hope for the church. If they really live in unity with the local church and the universal church, they will be a real expression of communion and a means for constructing a still deeper communion. Their fidelity to their mission will depend on how careful they are to educate their members in the fullness of the Christian faith through listening to the word of God, fidelity to the teaching of the magisterium, to the hierarchical order of the church, and to the sacramental life. If this condition is fulfilled, their experience, rooted in a commitment to the

complete liberation of humankind, becomes a treasure for the whole church [no. 69].

At the same time, we should like to have seen in the Instruction a fuller development of this new presence of the poor both in Latin American society and in the Christian community.

The base ecclesial communities are undoubtedly one of the most fruitful forces at work in the Latin American church. They have their place in the broad channel cut out by the council in its reflections on the people of God and its historical journey. They are a manifestation of the people of God as existing in the world of poverty but at the same time they are profoundly marked by Christian faith. They reveal the presence in the church of the "nobodies" of history or, to use another expression of the council, of a "messianic people" (*Lumen Gentium*, no. 9). They are, in other words, a people journeying through history and continually bringing about the messianic reversal—"the last shall be first"—that is a key element in every truly liberating process.[143]

A Christian Praxis

I discussed the meaning and scope of the term "praxis" in part 1 of this essay. *Libertatis Conscientia* (and *Libertatis Nuntius* as well) uses the word several times and in its final chapter relates it to the church's social teaching. Especially interesting in this chapter are the frequent citations of John Paul II's encyclical on human work, which has brought a new vision to many aspects of this field.[144] For the encyclical does not limit itself to pointing out one or another social problem but shows that in this area we are dealing with a real *economic and social system* that is built on the priority of capital over labor.

The deepest meaning of praxis is love and justice.[145] *Libertatis Conscientia* speaks of praxis as "the putting into practice of the great commandment of love. This is the supreme principle of Christian social morality, founded upon the gospel and the whole of tradition since apostolic times and the age of the fathers of the church up to and including the recent statements of the magisterium" (no. 71).

The issue is indeed social morality and not political programs.

The latter are not the church's business: "The political and economic running of society is not a direct part of its mission" (*LC*, no. 61). The church's social teaching "has established itself as a doctrine by using the resources of human wisdom and the sciences. It concerns the ethical aspect of this life. It takes into account the technical aspects of problems but always in order to judge them from the moral point of view" (no. 72).[146]

It is very interesting to see how this teaching is always presented in a way that is open to new questions. Rightly so, for the ground on which it is located is especially changeable. *Libertatis Nuntius* therefore says: "This teaching is by no means closed. It is, on the contrary, open to all the new questions that are so numerous today. In this perspective, the contribution of theologians and other thinkers in all parts of the world to the reflection of the church is indispensable today" (XI, 12). *Libertatis Conscientia* repeats the thought in very clear terms: "being essentially orientated toward action, this teaching develops in accordance with the changing circumstances of history. This is why, together with principles that are always valid, it also involves contingent judgments. Far from constituting a closed system, it remains open to new questions that continually arise; it requires the contribution of all charisms, experiences, and skills" (no. 72).

The texts are clear and expressive. We are dealing with a changing subject matter, and factual judgments are therefore contingent; the important thing is to proceed in fidelity to the permanent ethical requirements of the kingdom of life and to the concrete life of persons in society.

The right to property provides a clear example of the approach taken by a social morality that is always open to new situations. The nature of the present essay does not allow me to review the teachings of the church on this subject.[147] I shall simply remind the reader that the treatment of the subject by the fathers of the church is dominated by consideration for the "right of the poor" — that is, the right to life, which is God's gift. In Thomas Aquinas we find in more technical form distinctions that had begun to emerge centuries before:

> The institution of private property is legitimate, but only
> by a secondary natural right and not by a primary natural

right as such. In other words, St. Thomas gave private property a relative justification, in which he combined the idea of every human being's natural right and not by a primary natural right as such. In other words, St. Thomas gave private property a relative justification, in which he combined the idea of every human being's natural right of *dominium* over things and considerations on the appropriateness of a distribution of property among human beings with the intention that it also be correctly administered for the good of all.[148]

This passage describes, appropriately, the level at which the right of private property is located. In the social teaching of the church private property has always been looked upon as the material setting for the exercise of personal freedom. But this freedom itself implies relationships. Therefore because private property derives from the right of all to the goods of this world and because it is meant as an aid to a freedom that, as socially exercised, implies bonds with other persons, private property too will always have a social function. This is a classic element in the teaching of the church,[149] but in recent years John XXIII and Paul VI have laid special stress on it.

As early as the Puebla Conference, John Paul II referred to "the church's teaching, which says that there is a *social mortgage* on all private property" (Opening Address, III, 4). He subsequently returned often to this theme. His most forceful statement on the subject is his encyclical on human work. Here the primacy of human beings over the fruits of their work makes possible a strong and penetrating critique of every type of liberalism and collectivism that repudiates, in fact or in principle, the value of the human person.

There is no need of insisting on the danger of an individualist conception that regards profit as the driving force of economic activity or on that of a totalitarian vision that disregards the freedom of each person. The statements in my writings on the social appropriation of the means of production (which does not necessarily mean state ownership, although this may be the form it takes in some cases) are intended as a response to the first danger. In like manner (I have already referred to this), my statement about the social appropriation of freedom was meant to counteract an individualist approach, but also to meet the second danger just mentioned—that is, the failure to allow for the personal freedom of *all* members of a society.

Justice and freedom are two requirements of a human society. In this realm of ideas, many think that a healthy balance between private ownership, social ownership, and state ownership can be a good way of meeting and promoting these two requirements. But here we are certainly in the presence of what *Libertatis Conscientia* calls "contingent judgments." It is important, for this reason, to be always open to "the new questions that continually arise." The concrete forms may vary, but they will always have to maintain the right to life that finds expression in the right to use the goods of this world, together with all that flows from them, and the right to personal freedom.

Given the present situation in Latin America, the social aspect is very important for liberation theology. But it is precisely that: *one aspect* in a theological approach that covers other fields. Because liberation theology is a reflection on the faith, it must be attentive to many other aspects of the Christian message. Furthermore, it must always bear in mind:

> Emphasis on the practice of justice and on solidarity with the poor must never become an obsession and prevent our seeing that this commitment reveals its value and ultimate meaning only within the vast and mysterious horizon of God's gratuitous love. Furthermore, the very building of a just society requires a stimulus and an enveloping atmosphere that gratuitousness alone can supply [*On Job*, p. 96].

The social teaching of the church deals with the ethical implications of social problems and is the work of the magisterium. Liberation theology, like every theology, is a discourse on the entire Christian message and is not backed by the authority of the church's teaching office. There can therefore be no question of opting for the one or the other.

THE PREFERENTIAL OPTION FOR THE POOR

Our present consciousness of the preferential option for the poor has its origin in the life of the church in Latin America

(see its theology and its magisterium). Moreover, this consciousness emerged after Vatican II, as the final report of the 1985
synod clearly acknowledges:

> Following the Second Vatican Council the church became
> more aware of its mission in the service of the poor, the
> oppressed, and the outcast. In this preferential option,
> which must not be understood as exclusive, the true spirit
> of the gospel shines forth. Jesus Christ declared the poor
> blessed (Mt. 5:3; Lk. 6:20), and he himself wished to be
> poor for us (2 Cor. 8:9) [II, D, 6].

This thought is abundantly present in church documents of
recent years. As *Libertatis Conscientia* says very aptly, "The special option for the poor, far from being a sign of particularism
or sectarianism, manifests the universality of the church's being
and mission" (no. 68).[150] This has been the constant position of
liberation theology and of the magisterium since Medellín.[151]

Our present awareness of this theme is simply the result of
a new reading of a central element in the Christian message, an
element that has its roots in the Bible and permeates the life of
the church.[152] This new reading, moreover, is a condition of the
way we understand that element today.

The God of the Kingdom

The God whom Jesus proclaims is the God of the kingdom.
The kingdom expresses God's will, which Jesus says is his food
and which we ask may "be done" when we pray the prayer he
taught us. The God of the Bible is inseparable from God's will,
from God's kingdom; any attempt to invoke and encounter God
while divorcing God from the kingdom amounts to making an
idol and adoring a god different from the God of Jesus Christ.
A god without a kingdom is a fetish and the work of our own
hands (see Is. 44:14–17).

To the question echoed by the psalmist, "Where is your
God?" (Ps. 42:10), the gospel of Jesus replies: "In the kingdom."
But during the time when we await the Lord's parousia, God's
presence in history makes itself known only in an unobtrusive
way that necessitates a spiritual discernment. The Bible often

refers to God as a hidden God. "He came to his own home, and his own people received him not" (Jn. 1:11). Christ makes himself present precisely through those who are "absent" from history, those who are not invited to the banquet (see Lk. 14:15–24), those who are not the great ones of the world, the respected, "the wise and understanding" (Mt. 11:25). The "absent" are the poor, the hungry, and those who weep, according to Luke, who then goes on to contrast them with the rich, the sated, and those who laugh (Lk. 6:14–25). All these descriptions of Luke refer to real persons and concrete situations.[153] The "absent" also include "tax collectors and prostitutes," persons who are public sinners and therefore outcast and despised.

It is not only the rejected, but those also who are called to the kingdom, who will ask: "When did we give you food or drink, or visit you in prison?" (see Mt. 25:37–45). By identifying himself with the poor of the world, the Lord to some extent hides his face and activity behind them, thereby telling us that the casting out of the poor is a denial of the kingdom and causes his absence.

The task of the church is to proclaim the kingdom of God and thus combat the idolatry that consists in separating God from the reign of God. One part of its mission that it cannot evade is to point to the absence of God when justice is not done to the poor. Along this line, Medellín said: "Where this social peace does not exist, there will we find social, political, economic, and cultural inequalities, there will we find rejection of the peace of the Lord, and a rejection of the Lord himself" (*Peace*, no. 14c). The other side of the church's mission is to recognize and proclaim the hidden presence of God in history. Therefore, going beyond social analysis (which is necessary) to what Christians see as really at stake in the Latin American situation, Puebla says: "This situation of pervasive extreme poverty takes on very concrete faces in real life. In these faces we ought to recognize the suffering features of Christ the Lord, who questions and challenges us" (no. 31).

The perception and discernment of this connection between God and the poor is an essential responsibility of the church, for its task is to proclaim God's kingdom as inchoately present in history. The kingdom is the first and last word on the meaning of history, and all human beings are called to it. For this reason, the poor (the dispossessed, the starving, the afflicted), who have a privileged place in the kingdom, must also have a privileged place in the historical task of the church.[154] Unless this privileged place is acknowledged, it is not possible to grasp the meaning and requirements of universality; universality in turn places the predilection for the poor in its proper context.

In this realm of ideas, when we say that the church is the sacrament of universal salvation, we are saying (to put it in biblical terms) that the church is the sign of the presence of the kingdom of God who is at work in human history (see Puebla, no. 227). This kingdom, therefore, cannot be understood apart from the preference Christ shows for the poor as he reveals to us the Father's universal love. In this tension between preference and universality resides the richness and originality of the Christian message.

The privileged place of the poor in the kingdom of God lays demands on a church that is called to be the sacrament of the kingdom's presence in history. The gift of the kingdom stands in judgment on the activity of the church as the community of the followers of Jesus.

Awareness of this truth has led to study of the biblical meaning of poverty as a means of understanding ecclesial existence and action. Many works have been devoted to the subject in recent years; they make clear the cruel contrast between, on the one hand, the experience of premature and unjust *death* entailed in the poverty in which the vast majority of the human race are living, and, on the other, the kingdom of *life* that Jesus proclaims. This contrast makes the question of a church of the poor something more than simply a question of sensitivity to social wretchedness or of a struggle for social justice and the building of a new social and political order. Or, to phrase it more accurately, when we adopt the viewpoint of a church of the poor, we locate these legitimate demands in their true context: at the heart of the Christian message—that is, in relation to the God of life.

According to the Bible, "to live" is always "to live with," "to live for," "to be present to others"—that is, it implies communion. Death is utter aloneness. That is why lepers, who in Jesus' time were cut off from the community, were regarded as dead;

healing restored them to life, not only because they were cured of an infirmity but also because they could now return to the human community. It is very probable that the debated name "Yahweh" belongs in such a context and means: I am he who is with you; I am life.[155] *Libertatis Conscientia* says:

> The situation of the poor is a situation contrary to the covenant. This is why the law of the covenant protects them by means of precepts that reflect the attitude of God when God liberated Israel from the slavery of Egypt. Injustice to the little ones and the poor is a grave sin, which destroys communion with God [no. 46].

The point is well made. The meaning and demands of the kingdom confront the church in a radical way with the question of poverty that results from an unjust situation. I am not saying that the realities of history do not also challenge the church. The point I want to emphasize here is that the Christian community can face up to these realities with all their demands only if it relates them to the Father's will to love and life. The ultimate reason for the option for the poor lies in the God in whom we believe.[156] There can be, and are, other reasons for the option, but in the final analysis solidarity with the dispossessed and exploited—in their life and in their death—is anchored in our faith in God: the God of life who is not revealed among the dead, but among the living (Lk. 24:5).

Christians are witnesses to the resurrection, to the gift of life that definitively conquers death. Testimony to the Lord's resurrection is situated between acceptance of the grace of the kingdom and the historical demands that this grace makes. The task of the church is located precisely between these two terms. The church is called to be a sign of the life of the kingdom within history and to make that life a reality, thus placing itself under the judgment of the word of God. If the issue raised by the poverty of the majority of humankind is, in the last analysis, the choice between life and death, then the challenge facing us is not simply that of a "social problem," in the sense of something more or less accidental from the viewpoint of the fundamental demands of the gospel message. No, what we are confronting is something contrary to the kingdom of life that Jesus Christ proclaims.

In view of all this, were the church to refuse the preferential option for the poor (in the framework of God's universal love), it would be denying that it is a gathered people animated by the power of the Spirit.

The Church of the Beatitudes

According to *Libertatis Conscientia*, "the Beatitudes . . . enable us to situate the temporal order in relation to a transcendent order, which gives the temporal order its true measure, but without taking away its own nature" (no. 62). We must ask why they have this function.

As everyone knows, we have two versions of the Beatitudes: one in the Gospel of Luke, the other in the Gospel of Matthew.[157] The divergence between them has given rise to many commentaries and observations. The first Beatitude sets the tone for both the similarities and the differences. Luke has: "Blessed are you poor"; Matthew adds a phrase: "Blessed are the poor in spirit"; according to both, "yours (theirs) is the kingdom of God (heaven)." Has Matthew "spiritualized" Luke's version?

Some commentators think so. On the other hand, no one can deny that the Gospel of Matthew is notably insistent on the need for concrete and "material" actions toward others and especially toward the poor (see Mt. 25:31–46). This emphasis does not seem to be compatible with a supposed Matthean "spiritualism." The seeming contradiction between the two approaches to the Beatitudes is perhaps the result of an application to the first Gospel of categories that do not do justice to the originality of its outlook. Let us try to enter into the outlook.

In Luke, the first Beatitude refers to the real poor, those poor in material things, the poor of whom I have been speaking in this essay. Of whom would Matthew have us think when he speaks of "the poor in spirit"?

In the biblical outlook (and the Semitic outlook generally), "spirit" is something dynamic: breath, vital force. The dynamism finds expression in knowledge, understanding, virtue, and decision-making. Spirit is the dynamic aspect of the human being.

The Old Testament often uses the expression "in spirit" as an addition that changes the basic meaning of certain words and gives them a figurative meaning. In Proverbs 16:18, for example, the words "lofty in spirit" are to be translated as "haughty"; in Isaiah 29:24 "erring in spirit" refers to one who has gone astray. "Poor in spirit" is a comparable expression and means something more than a lack of, or detachment from, material goods.

The verse in Matthew has at times been translated "blessed are they who choose to be poor." The intention is to avoid the spiritualist interpretation mentioned above, but, despite the good intention, the expression is somewhat defective and an ambiguity remains. On the positive side, the choice of poverty brings out the dynamic aspect of Christian life as seen in solidarity with the people at the bottom of the historical scale. On the negative side, I think that spiritual poverty refers to a situation that is more basic and more comprehensive than the choice of real poverty.

Spiritual poverty means spiritual childhood, which is a key idea in the gospel. It comprises complete availability to the Lord and the recognition that the Father's will is our food, as Jesus says in the Gospel of John. Spiritual childhood is the attitude of those who know themselves to be sons and daughters of God, and brothers and sisters of their fellow human beings.

"Poor in spirit" is a synonym for "disciple of Christ." The other seven Beatitudes of Matthew spell out various attitudes proper to those who are followers of the Lord. They display a peculiar characteristic of this Gospel: the emphasis on ethical requirements: to be pleasant to others (this is the meaning of "meek" or "mild"), to practice justice, to be merciful, to be a peacemaker, and so on.

In the perspective just explained (poor in spirit = disciples), it makes sense to say that Christians should choose a poor lifestyle. The reason is not that being poor is an ideal to be striven for but that to be a disciple *today* includes being in solidarity with the real poor, those who lack the necessities for living in the way that their dignity as human beings and children of God calls for. As Medellín reminds us, poverty according to the Bible is an evil, a situation not desired by the God of life.

It will be helpful here to look at the key role played by the

theme of justice in the Matthean Beatitudes (see 5:6 and 5:10).
As *Libertatis Conscientia* says,

> Read and interpreted in their full context, the Beatitudes
> express the spirit of the kingdom of God, which is to come.
> But, in the light of the definitive destiny of humankind
> thus manifested, there simultaneously appear with a more
> vivid clarity the foundations of justice in the temporal
> order [no. 62].

It is not possible, in effect, to separate these two questions.

The establishment of justice and right is a central theme of
the Old Testament, and we find it in countless passages of the
Bible. The word "justice" has a twofold meaning: it is a gift of
God, but it also implies a relationship between human beings.
It is therefore the work of God, but it is likewise the work of
the king, of the people, and of believers generally. It is both gift
and task. The two aspects are closely connected. It is in the
relationship between human beings that the gift of God's justice
receives its historical embodiment.

Seen against this backdrop, the idea of justice proves to be
extremely important and fruitful for the interpretation of the
Beatitudes. In Matthew's Gospel we find seven mentions of justice, five of them in the Sermon on the Mount.[158] In the Beatitudes themselves, justice occupies a key place.

If we look closely at the Beatitudes in Matthew, it is easy to
see that they are divided into two distinct groups.[159] The first
group is inspired directly by Luke (or Luke's source) and ends
with the fourth Beatitude: "Blessed are those who hunger and
thirst for righteousness." The second group is Matthew's own
contribution and does not have the element of contrast that the
Beatitudes have in Luke. This second group also ends with a
mention of justice (righteousness) in its relation to the gift of
the kingdom: "Blessed are those who are persecuted for righteousness' sake, for theirs is the kingdom of heaven."

The practice of justice is required of the disciples of Christ.
Therefore they are blessed if they desire ("hunger and thirst")
to establish it, and they are blessed as well if they are persecuted
because of it. The connection between the kingdom of God and

the justice God requires is a close one throughout the Sermon on the Mount, where we find this important and indeed decisive verse: "Seek first his kingdom and his righteousness, and all these things shall be yours as well" (Mt. 6:33). As the preceding verse (32) shows, the kingdom and its justice are from the Father, and this explains their primacy in Christian life.

The practice of justice by the disciple finds expression in life-giving actions in behalf of the neighbor and especially the most defenseless: the poor. Matthew is careful to point this out in a passage that is part of the unit in which the Beatitudes are found.

The passage on the Beatitudes ends with v. 12, but what follows is fully integrated with it. Disciples are persons called to bear witness by concrete actions. What they do must be seen by others in order that the latter may receive the message of the Beatitudes. "Good works" (5:16) is a technical expression in the Bible; it refers to "works of mercy," which are enumerated for us, in a now classic list, in Matthew 25:31–46. The visibility of these good works ("light," "lamp") is not for the sake of personal ostentation; they are to be done for the glory of God. This glorification is the ultimate purpose of the works done by the disciples of Jesus; through these works human beings are to be led to the Father. To glorify the Father means to acknowledge the primacy of his love, to adhere to his will, to be faithful to his plan for the human race.

The works done by disciples are their way of reaching the Father; in this manner they make their own the way taken by Christ. The passage on the Beatitudes really ends with v. 16 and shows us the role played by works in the attitudes proper to followers of Jesus. "Blessed are the poor in spirit" and the other Beatitudes mean: Blessed are the disciples, those who practice justice by works of love and life, and who thereby glorify the Father. This approach to the Beatitudes makes it possible to establish a fruitful relationship between the beginning of Matthew 5, where the preaching of Jesus starts, and Matthew 25, where that preaching ends. Blessed are the disciples, because they give food to the hungry and drink to the thirsty, and because they clothe the naked and visit the prisoner; in other words, because by means of concrete actions they give life and thus proclaim the kingdom.[160]

The Beatitudes in Luke put the emphasis on the gratuitousness of the love of God, who has a predilection for the poor. The Beatitudes in Matthew fill out the picture by specifying the ethical requirements that flow from this loving initiative of God. The two approaches are complementary. Matthew does not "spiritualize" the Beatitudes; rather, if I may coin a word, he "disciple-izes" them. The Matthean approach is especially demanding: the followers of Jesus are those who translate the grace they have received into works for the neighbor and especially the poor; on this account they are called blessed and fitted to enter the kingdom "prepared for you from the foundation of the world" (Mt. 25:34).

The life of disciples unfolds between gratuitousness and demand. In the passage on the Beatitudes Matthew stresses the need of specific behavior toward others. Such behavior is a requirement flowing from the gift of the kingdom. Nothing makes greater demands of us for solidarity with others than the gratuitousness of God's love. The church of the poor is the church of the Beatitudes, a church committed to the poor and oppressed of this world and, at the same time, completely bent on proclaiming the gratuitous love of God.

CHURCH OF THE POOR

The challenge of poverty comes to the church from the present situation; at a deeper level, however, it comes from God. The Beatitudes are not simply a text on the poor; they are a revelation concerning God and God's unmerited love. As Puebla makes clear, this love, expressed in the work of the Son, is the reason why "the poor merit preferential attention, whatever may be the moral or personal situation in which they find themselves" (no. 1142).[161]

The place occupied by the poor in the kingdom we are to proclaim has led persons to speak of "a church of the poor." This approach has been subject to various and at times disputed interpretations (see *LN*, IX, 9–13). It will be worthwhile, therefore, to recall the setting of the initial insights on this subject and to retrace the path followed by this idea and this ecclesial experience.

John XXIII and Vatican II

John XXIII raised the question of the church of the poor in a somewhat surprising form, in a message delivered a month before the sessions of Vatican II began (September 11, 1962). He reminds us that Christ is our light and that it is with him as its point of departure that the church must serve human beings. For this purpose he indicates some important points: the equality of all peoples in the exercise of their rights and duties; the defense of the family; the obligation to reject individualism and accept responsibility for society. The pope adds: "A further luminous point: confronted with the underdeveloped countries, the church presents itself as it is and wants to be, as the church of all, and particularly, the church of the poor." A few lines further on, he speaks of "the miseries of social life that cry out for vengeance in the sight of God."[162]

Universality and Preference. In the passage just cited, Pope John XXIII, first of all, links the church and the poor countries. The way he does it is significant. In his *Mater et Magistra* he had spoken of "developing" countries; here he drops this milder expression and speaks directly of "underdeveloped countries." He is talking to the real poverty of the vast majority of the human race; this state of affairs challenges the church to take new stock of itself.

From the outset, then, he raises a question he considers to be pregnant with consequences for ecclesiology. The situation of misery and injustice in which the poor live is not simply a matter for concern on the part of the church or for measures to alleviate it. Rather it represents a challenge to that renewal of ecclesial self-knowledge to which Paul VI would emphatically summon the church a short time later. John XXIII thus cuts to the heart of the relationship between poverty and the church apart from which any concern of the church for the situation of the poor is likely to be considered provisional and, in the final analysis, extraneous to its mission and its real being. John XXIII avoids this danger because in this same message he situates himself in the perspective of liberation in Christ and of the nearness of God's reign (he refers in this context to Lk. 21:20–33).

Secondly, the passage indicates the two poles of an important tension, which we have already mentioned. It begins by saying that the church is (and wants to be) the church *of all*: this is a clear statement that the church's task embraces the whole world. The reign of God embraces all; no one is excluded from it. The Christian community is an expression of this love (its sacrament in history, to use the council's words) and therefore reaches out to every human being without exception.

It is significant that the passage begins with this statement and thus provides a proper and fruitful setting for the other pole of the tension — namely, that the church is (and wants to be) the church particularly *of the poor*. This particularism, this predilection (which obviously does not mean exclusiveness) is not opposed, in the pope's understanding of it, to universality, but rather gives universality a demanding concrete form in history. The God proclaimed by Jesus Christ is a God whose call is universal and directed to every human being, but *at the same time* a God who has a preferential love for the poor and the dispossessed. The dialectic of universality and particularity is a key to understanding the Christian message and the God who is revealed in it.

Finally, John XXIII presents the church, thus viewed, as something that is in process of becoming. As I just pointed out, he twice says that the church "is and wants to be." The situation is not cut and dried. The church is not yet everything it ought to be; it has a journey to make through history. John XXIII shows the direction the journey must take, and without any triumphalism (as Christians would say during the period of the council) acknowledges what remains to be done.

The passage I have been analyzing is a short one but every word in it counts. Its restraint and moderation must not make us overlook its generative power. The words, backed by the witness of that free spirit, John XXIII, marked the beginning of a movement, a process with advances and setbacks, that is still going on, because it has not deployed all its virtualities.

On the Way of Poverty. As everyone knows, the first session of the council brought a revolution in the ways the church had been following until that time. As a result of the richly creative ferment of ideas whose proponents were trying to reflect as faithfully as possible the insights of John XXIII, numerous paths were opened up that transformed current patterns of thinking and acting. At the end of this first stage of the council, Cardinal Lercaro, archbishop of Bologna, gave a memorable address on the theme of the church of the poor. It deserves detailed analysis, but I shall limit myself to two points.

With great clarity and prophetic vision, Cardinal Lercaro said: "If we treat this subject of winning the poor for the gospel as just another one of the many themes that must occupy the attention of the council we shall not satisfy the most real and most profound exigencies of our day (including our great hope of furthering the unity of all Christendom)." And he added: "The church herself is in truth the theme of the council [especially insofar as] she is above all 'the church of the poor.' "[163]

The passage is very clear and endeavors to be faithful to the first two themes set down by John XXIII: the needs of our time and the unity of Christians. To achieve this goal (according to the cardinal) the attention of the council must be focused on the third of the pope's themes: the church of the poor.

A second point emerges from the address on which I am commenting. Cardinal Lercaro's outlook is profoundly theological, not because he is insensitive to the social dimension of poverty but because he is bent on placing the mystery of Christ at the center of the discussion. He said: "The Mystery of Christ in the church is always, but particularly today, the Mystery of Christ in the poor, since the church, as Pope John XXIII has said, is truly the church of all, but is particularly 'the church of the poor.' " He therefore thinks that the absence of this essential aspect of the Christian message is a serious defect in the provisional schemata presented to the council.[164] The situation of the poor must be related not only to the social teaching of the church but also and above all to the light of Christ and his reign. Given the archbishop's approach, it is not surprising that in his view the other two themes of John XXIII—openness to the world and Christian unity—required making the theme of the church of the poor a central concern of the council.

Some task forces were set up to deal with these ideas, and they were very active in the corridors of the council. No. 8 of *Lumen Gentium* seeks to include these concerns in a rich but brief christological statement. Then there is the fine passage in *Ad Gentes*, no. 5, though it is even shorter, and a few allusions scattered through the other documents. I should like to call attention to two important ideas.

The two texts just mentioned carefully make Christ the focus of their treatment of poverty. Both refer to the evangelization of the poor, and *Lumen Gentium* bases this mandate on the fact that the image of the Lord is to be seen in the poor. Puebla will take over this idea and give it beautiful and powerful expression (nos. 31–39).

Both texts speak of poverty as a "way" that Christ followed and that the church too must follow on its pilgrimage through history. Poverty is thus not a goal or an ideal but a means of giving authentically evangelical witness.

These conciliar perspectives made room for experiments and thinking along the lines of "the church of the poor." The insight of John XXIII would be taken over in the life and thinking of the Latin American church.

Sacrament of Salvation in a Poor World

Vatican II spoke of the church as a "universal sacrament of salvation." What is required of the church if it is to be a universal sacrament of salvation in a world stamped by poverty and injustice? This is the great question the council puts to many Latin American Christians. Medellín was an effort to answer it, as was Puebla later on.

Poor with the Poor. The first problem is to take a stand on the "inhuman wretchedness" (Medellín, *Poverty*, no. 1) I mentioned earlier. The situation these two words describe has to be analyzed not only in its effects but also in its causes, so that they can be eliminated.[165] The situation in which the reign of life must be proclaimed is one of difficulty and conflict, and "represents a serious challenge to the evangelizing work of the church" (*Documento*, no. 16). Puebla therefore says that in Latin

America we have opted for "a church that is a sacrament of communion, a church that, in a history marked by conflicts, contributes irreplaceable energies to promote the reconciliation and solidarity of our peoples" (no. 1302).

This supposes, however, what the council glimpsed: that the church travels the "way of poverty" (*Ad Gentes*, no. 5; Flannery, p. 818). The church must be what Medellín calls a "poor church"—that is, a church that in order to be a sacrament of salvation involves itself with the poor and with poverty: "The poverty of the church is, in effect, a constant factor in the history of salvation" (*Poverty*, no. 5). This involvement will require a denunciation of "the unjust lack of this world's goods and the sin that begets it," and an ability to preach and live in "spiritual poverty, as an attitude of spiritual childhood and openness to the Lord" (ibid.).[166]

This perspective gave rise in Latin America during those years to many commitments and experiments by local churches, Christian communities, and religious families that wanted to bear witness to liberation in Christ in the midst of the poor. The task was not an easy one. That is why Puebla would speak of the necessity of a "conversion" of individual Christians and of the church as a whole: "We affirm the need for conversion on the part of the whole church to a preferential option for the poor, an option aimed at their integral liberation" (no. 1134). The idea of a "preferential option for the poor" is added six more times in the Puebla document. What the phrase calls for is a radical change of outlook, a change that cannot come about except by a gradual process. The pursuit of it brings advances but also pitfalls, enthusiasms and discouragements, successes and failures.

This preference for the poor must find expression in an authentic "solidarity with the poor ... [which] means that we make ours their problems and their struggles, that we know how to speak with them" (Medellín, *Poverty*, no. 10). The requirement of solidarity would put its seal on the practice of the church after Medellín (see *Drink*, pp. 95ff.). John Paul II would later repeat the same theme in a very powerful way, speaking of the church's solidarity with the poor as "its mission, its service, a proof of its fidelity to Christ." Then, using an expression of John

XXIII not heard for a long time in magisterial documents at this high level, the pope added that the purpose of this solidarity is "so that it can truly be the 'church of the poor'" (*LE*, no. 8).[167]

From the beginning, however, it was also understood that preference for the poor must not lead to forgetfulness of another basic principle of the gospel: the universality of Christian love. Consequently, after speaking of solidarity with the poor, Medellín went on to say that the Church must be "the humble servant of all our people" (*Poverty*, no. 8).[168] Later on, Puebla repeated this point, drawing its inspiration from Medellín and the theology being developed in Latin America during those years.

Because of Christ. The theme of the church of the poor has a clearly christological dimension which leads to Medellín and crystalizes around its documents. In other words, there is no question simply of being sensitive to the concrete situation of the poor who make up the vast majority in Latin America; the fundamental call is rather to faith in Christ, which is to give full meaning to everything. Medellín's statement on poverty makes this unmistakably clear. Of many relevant passages in it, I shall cite only one: "The poverty of so many brothers cries out for justice, solidarity, open witness, commitment, strength, and exertion *directed* to the fulfillment of the redeeming mission to which it [the church] is committed by Christ" (*Poverty*, no. 7, italics added). The salvation that Christ brings and of which the church is a sacrament within history is what gives meaning to the whole issue of "the church of the poor." "Christian poverty, an expression of love, is solidarity *with the poor* and is a protest *against* poverty. This is the concrete, contemporary meaning of the witness of poverty. It is a poverty lived not for its own sake, but rather as an authentic imitation of Christ; it is a poverty that means taking on the sinful human condition to liberate humankind from sin and all its consequences" (*Liberation*, p. 172).

Libertatis Conscientia also stresses this christological perspective:

Christ was foretold by the prophets as the messiah of the poor; and it was among the latter, the humble, the "poor

of Yahweh," who were thirsting for the justice of the kingdom, that he found hearts ready to receive him. But he
also wished to be near to those who, though rich in the
goods of this world, were excluded from the community as
"publicans and sinners," for he had come to call them to
conversion [no. 66].

That exclusion places them in a situation of marginalization
and scorn on the part of the politically and religiously powerful.
This christological outlook is also inspired by another statement of Vatican II. In *Lumen Gentium*, no. 8, the council says
that the church "recognizes in those who are poor and who
suffer the image of its poor and suffering founder . . . and in
them it strives to serve Christ." This identification of Christ with
the poor (see Mt. 25:31–46) is a principal theme in reflection
on the church of the poor. This was the very heart of John
XXIII's insight ("the church is, and wants to be"), as developed
by Cardinal Lercaro. It is important to call attention to this point
because there is a tendency to see the whole issue as a "social
problem" and to think that one has grasped the full significance
of poverty for the church when one is concerned about social
issues.

That is not how "the church of the poor" is understood in
Latin America. The approach taken by the church there manifests a profound fidelity to John XXIII and to the imprint his
ideas left on the council.[169]

Christian and Ecclesial Identity

The "church of the poor" represents an ecclesial outlook with
a long history behind it. St. Paul was able to express it with
unsurpassed power. To the church that lived in the important
and wealthy city of Corinth the Apostle wrote:

Consider your call, brethren; not many of you were wise
according to worldly standards, not many were powerful,
not many were of noble birth; but God chose what is foolish in the world to shame the wise, God chose what is weak
in the world to shame the strong, God chose what is low
and despised in the world, even things that are not, to bring

to nothing things that are, so that no human being might boast in the presence of God [1 Cor. 1:26–29].

In order to glimpse God's predilection for the poor the Corinthians had only to look around them in the Christian community. There is a reference here to historical experience (2 Cor. 8:2 speaks of the "extreme poverty" of the communities in Macedonia). But this passage of Paul gives a theological reading of this experience and expresses an understanding of the church that has an authentic and more demanding point of reference: God. God's mercy and will to life reveal themselves in God's preference for what the world considers foolish and weak, for what is common and scorned, for "things that are not." The gratuitousness of God's love is shown in the confounding and humbling of the wise, the strong, and "the things that are."

The church of the poor in Corinth sets the standard for us: the proclamation of the kingdom of God requires, and feeds, a language for speaking about God. It is the church's task to talk about God by its actions and words. The gospel says that the Spirit will inspire the community of disciples and tell them what they must say in bearing witness to Jesus Christ.

This discourse about God must have its basis in a life of commitment to the situation of poverty as well as in solidarity with efforts to achieve freedom from the injustice that poverty embodies. It is in these conditions that the vast majority of the human family live (the despised races, the exploited classes, the marginalized cultures, women discriminated against). Their experience must be translated for the followers of Jesus into a mystical language about God that recognizes the presence and fulness of God's gratuitous love, but it must also find expression in a prophetic language about God the liberator who rebels against the unjust death of the poor. The combination of these two languages will enable us to proclaim the God who is revealed in Jesus Christ.

The commitment of the church to the poor often elicits expressions of concern regarding the religious meaning of the church's mission: Will the church not be withdrawing from its proper task and, as a result, pay a high price: the loss of its identity? The church must indeed be always vigilant in these matters; I think, moreover, that nowadays there is a great need that the church assert its identity, not out of arrogance but out of fidelity to the Lord and his word, as well as out of a desire to serve in an authentic way all those to whom the universal love of God must be proclaimed. This identity is a necessary condition for establishing a saving dialogue.

But, far from adversely affecting its task in this world, solidarity with the poor leads the church to a better grasp of its own identity as sign of God's kingdom in history, for it will be better able to speak of the greatness of God and of God's preference for the disinherited of the earth.

When we say that the church must be a servant, we must think in the first place of service to God. But this is the God who is revealed as God precisely "by always taking a position, passionately and unconditionally, on this side and this side exclusively: against the proud and for the humble, against those who enjoy rights and privileges and for those who are denied and stripped of these rights."[170] The same point is made in a recent powerful text: "The situation of the poor today in a world in which unjust structures compel the majority of the human family to live in dehumanizing conditions should be a constant reminder to us that God takes the side of the poor, in accordance with the plan of salvation revealed in Jesus Christ, who came 'to preach good news to the poor' (Lk. 4:18)."[171]

The church has therefore not lost its identity but rather gained it. Its identity consists in being on the side of the God of Jesus Christ, who loves every person and has a predilection for the least: the poor. It has not lost its identity, if we keep in mind in this context what the pillars of the church asked Paul to do: "remember the poor" (Gal. 2:10).

It is true, of course, that we must pay a price in order to be a church of the poor. The price, however, is not the church's authentic being and activity. The price is personal freedom, reputation, physical and mental wholeness, residence in one's own country, and, in some cases, one's very life.

CONCLUSION

Liberation theology originates in an objective: to bring the message of Christ alive in and on the basis of situations in which massive and inhuman poverty reigns. Its aim is "reflection, based on the gospel and the experiences of men and women committed to the process of liberation in the oppressed and exploited lands of Latin America."[172]

Insofar as liberation theology is an understanding of the faith, it is necessarily located within the church and has a function therein. Theology is always an activity carried on in the ecclesial community; it is not a purely individual activity. In his message to the bishops of Brazil, John Paul II says that liberation theology "should constitute a new stage — in close connection with former ones — of the theological reflection initiated with the apostolic tradition and continued by the great fathers and doctors, by the ordinary and extraordinary magisterium and, in more recent years, by the rich patrimony of the church's social doctrine, expressed in documents from *Rerum Novarum* to *Laborem Exercens*" (no. 5). We must all contribute to this "new stage" and wager on its success.

In this essay I have tried to situate myself in the perspective of service to the church's proclamation of Christ as the truth who makes us free. As I reach the end, it becomes clear that the task is an open-ended one. There are many points that need to be dealt with and clarified. One of the great joys of theological work, and indeed of Christian life generally, is undoubtedly the realization that the gospel always has new things to say to us. Never, in theology, are we able to realize fully the *"Abba, Father,"* that the Spirit causes us to speak.

The task of liberation theology is one that we must carry out while daily sharing the life of a people who are experiencing an especially harsh situation. We in Peru are living in a time when contempt for human life is continually expressed in daily actions. The result is a very profound national crisis that demands all our energies.[173] The various forms of violence (structural, terrorist, and repressive) sow death where we as Christians must bear witness to the kingdom of life. This is the great challenge facing our church today. The responsibility laid on it is a source of tension but also, despite everything, of deep joy, because it can respond to the challenge only by getting down to what is essential: its hope in the Lord who conquered death by rising to new life.

NOTES

1. At the beginning of a recent careful study of the teaching of John Paul II on this subject, Carlos I. González, a professor at the Gregorian University in Rome, wrote with good reason: "It is distressing to see how so many Christians, who have no direct access to the many publications on 'liberation theology,' are confused when they read so many contradictory reports in the newspapers or in such periodicals as do come into their hands. . . . In fact, many people with no expertise in this area take positions dictated by motives that do not result from any careful investigation. How often I have read in the press of various countries precipitate announcements of the condemnation of this theology whenever the pope in one or other address (for example, the one he delivered at Piura on February 4, 1985) says something that can be used to confirm or rebut positions already taken!" ("La teología de la liberación a la luz del magisterio de Juan Pablo II en América Latina," *Gregorianum*, 67 [1986]: 5).

2. To the documents mentioned may be added other statements of the ecclesial magisterium; I shall pay special attention to the *Documento de la conferencia episcopal peruana sobre teología de la liberación* (October, 1984—henceforth *Documento*).

English translation of the documents already mentioned in the text: Instruction on Certain Aspects of the "Theology of Liberation," Instruction on Christian Freedom and Liberation, the Letter to Brazil's Bishops, may be found in Alfred Hennelly, editor, *Liberation Theology: A Documentary History* (Maryknoll, N.Y.: Orbis Books, 1989).

Translation of other documents to be mentioned further on: John Paul II, encyclical on human work (*Laborem Exercens*) (September 14, 1981), in *Origins*, 11 (1981–82): 225–44; John Paul II, encyclical on social concerns (*Sollicitudo Rei Socialis*) (December 30, 1987), in *Origins*, 17 (1987–88): 641–60; The Final Report of the Synod of Bishops, in *Origins*, 17 (1987–88): 444–50.

3. "Ad alta quota col prefetto della fede," *30 giorni* (May 1986), p. 9.

4. The pope goes on to speak of a special role to be played by the bishops of Brazil in this area: "I think that in this field the church in Brazil can play an important and at the same time delicate role: that of creating the space and conditions for the development of a theological reflection that fully adheres to the church's constant teaching on social matters and, at the same time, is suitable for inspiring an effective pastoral praxis in favor of social justice, equity, the observance of

human rights, the construction of a human society based on brother-hood, harmony, truth, and charity." This charge, John Paul II says, to an episcopate whose sympathy for liberation theology is well known, is important for all of Latin America and the world: "Such a function, if realized, will certainly be a service the church can render to the nation and to Latin America, as well as to many other world regions where similarly serious challenges present themselves."

5. Consequently, the second 1986 Instruction is not a superfluous document on a subject on which everything has already been said. Some people think of it in this way, which explains their lack of sympathy for the promised document. One constant and bitter critic of liberation theology in Brazil ended a recent article on the subject by saying: "All this makes a further Roman document inopportune; on the one hand, it will hardly be able to say anything new; on the other, it will cause many disappointments and open the way for many criticisms and mis-understandings" (J. F. Martins Terra, "Um documento positivo sobre a Teologia da libertação?" *Actualização*, nos. 193–94 [January-February 1986]: 81). This is not an isolated view but is frequently met with in Latin America in circles unfavorable to the outlook at work in libera-tion theology. These are the same circles that have received with chilly silence the new document from the Congregation for the Doctrine of the Faith.

6. See, in this context, the dissatisfaction summed up in M. Gran-dona's analysis of *Libertatis Conscientia*, which reflects a conservative liberalism: "Compromiso en Roma," *Vision*, May 1986.

7. Interview cited above (n. 2), p. 9.

8. *LN*, 1: "The powerful and almost irresistible aspiration that people have for liberation constitutes one of the principal signs of the times which the church has to examine and interpret in the light of the gospel." *LC*, 5: "The quest for freedom and the aspiration to liberation, which are among the principal signs of the times in the modern world, have their first source in the Christian heritage."

9. In my opinion, events and recent documents make it possible to avoid the danger that H. A. Parra calls "the risk of the hour" in these discussions—namely, the danger of "giving the impression that liberation theology is falling back into the familiar disputes of the schools, the stardom of the intellectuals, the old system of theological censures and notes, the dialogue that ignores the people" ("La teología de la liberación despues de la Instrucción," *Theologica Xaveriana*, 73 [October-December 1984]: 401).

10. *LC*, 4: "According to the command of Christ the Lord, the truth of the gospel must be presented to all people, and they have a

right to have it presented to them. Its proclamation, in the power of the Spirit, includes full respect for the freedom of each individual and the exclusion of every form of constraint or pressure."

11. Such an analysis has its place in, for example, the discussion of religious freedom. I have had occasion to deal with religious freedom from this angle in past years; see G. Gutiérrez, "Libertad religiosa y diálogo salvador," in *Salvacion y construcción del mundo* (Barcelona: Editorial Nova Terra, 1968), and "Freedom and Salvation," in G. Gutiérrez and R. Shaull, *Liberation and Change* (Atlanta: John Knox, 1977).

12. This dialogue is also being carried on in the other texts of the present book.

13. In the pages that follow I shall also take into account Msgr. R. Durand's book, *Observaciones a Teología de la liberación y Fuerza Histórica de los Pobres* (Callao, 1985).

14. Karl Barth reminded us of this truth with incomparable energy.

15. In a perceptive article on this subject René Marlé comments on what European theology can learn from Latin American theology: "If there is one benefit which French theology can and ought to derive from liberation theology, it is the reminder of the ecclesial and social function of theology. A very elementary lesson, of course, but one worthwhile learning again in the form of a 'reading of the situation' and in a country in which theology has for a long time been marginalized and tempted to doubt its own importance." He adds, quite accurately: "Furthermore, at the same time that the liberation theologians are successfully reawakening the French consciousness of the social function of theology, they are awakening it to Christianity itself" ("Théologiens en procès," *Recherches de sciences religieuses* [January-March, 1986]: 95).

16. See G. Gutiérrez, *On Job. God-Talk and the Suffering of the Innocent*, (Maryknoll, N.Y.: Orbis Books, 1987 — henceforth *On Job*).

17. Lévi-Strauss's opinion on this point is revealing: "The author of this article has devoted his entire life to the pursuit of the social and human sciences. But he is not at all uncomfortable at having to recognize that no real parity can be established between these and the exact or natural sciences: the latter are sciences, the former are not. If we nonetheless use the same label for both, this is solely in virtue of a semantic fiction and a philosophical hope that has never received any confirmation" ("Critérios científicos de las disciplinas sociales y humanas," in *Aproximación al estructuralismo* [Buenos Aires: Editorial Galerna, 1967]: 57).

18. "Such a life [the life of contemplation] will be too high for

human attainment. It will not be lived by us in our merely human capacity but in virtue of something divine within us" (*The Ethics of Aristotle (The Nicomachean Ethics)* [Baltimore: Penguin Books, 1953], p. 305).

19. The following passage of Kant clearly shows the impact that the experimental sciences had on the way in which human understanding was conceived: "When Galilei experimented with balls of a definite weight on the inclined plane, when Torricelli caused the air to sustain a weight which he had calculated beforehand to be equal to that of a definite column of water, or when Stahl, at a later period, converted metals into lime, and reconverted lime into metal, by the addition and subtraction of certain elements; a light broke upon all natural philosophers. They learned that reason only perceives that which it produces after its own design; that it must not be content to follow, as it were, in the leading-strings of nature, but must proceed in advance with principles of judgment according to unvarying laws, and compel nature to reply to its questions. For accidental observations, made according to no preconceived plan, cannot be united under a necessary law. But it is this that reason seeks for and requires. It is only the principles of reason which can give to concordant phenomena the validity of laws, and it is only when experiment is directed by these rational principles that it can have any real utility. Reason must approach nature with the view, indeed, of receiving information from it, not, however, in the character of a pupil, who listens to all that his master chooses to tell him, but in that of a judge, who compels the witnesses to reply to those questions which he himself thinks fit to propose" (*Critique of Pure Reason*, Preface to the Second Edition, 1787 [Great Books of the Western World; Chicago: Encyclopaedia Britannica, 1952], p. 6).

20. See the historical survey of this theme in N. Lobkowicz, *Theory and Practice. History of a Concept from Aristotle to Marx* (Notre Dame, Ind.: University of Notre Dame Press, 1967).

21. *Power*, p. 60: "In insisting upon the truth as something lived, as something verified, we are not urging a merely mechanical conformity with the contemporary call for a link between knowledge and change. But the cultural world we live in does permit us to discover a point of departure, and new horizon, for theological reflection. This theology must now take a new route, and in order to do so it will have to appeal to its own fonts."

22. "We must not forget that the word of God issues its challenges. The scriptures are not a passive store of answers to our questions. We indeed read the Bible, but we can also say that the Bible 'reads us.' In many instances, our very questions will be reformulated" (G. Gutiérrez,

We Drink from Our Own Wells. The Spiritual Journey of a People [Mary-knoll, N.Y.: Orbis Books, 1984], p. 34. Henceforth *Drink*). For the same thought, see *On Job*, pp. xvii-xviii.

23. *Power*, 56. The passage continues: "From this point of departure, one can properly appreciate that Christians seek to understand their faith ultimately in function of 'the imitation of Christ'—which means feeling, thinking, and acting as did he. An authentic theology is always a 'spiritual theology,' as the fathers of the church understood spiritual theology. The life of faith, then, is not just a point of departure for theology. It is also its point of arrival. Belief and understanding have an annular relationship."

24. It is therefore clear that any use that theology may make of the culture of the age must be a critical use; theology is always a "critical reflection." The reason for this is that theology is a discourse on revelation and that this discourse has requirements specific to it. *LN* has reminded us of the necessity of this "critical examination of the analytical methods borrowed from other disciplines" (VII, 10). Along the same line, Cardinal Ratzinger spoke recently of "the presence in Marxism of elements of socio-economic analysis that can be used, though only critically and under certain conditions, in passing judgment on a social situation" (interview in *Herder-Korrespondenz*, August 1984, p. 365).

25. This intellectual approach to truth is often described as proper to and distinctive of the Greek spirit, although in fact it is only the philosophical expression of that culture. Other areas—literature and art, for example—in which the Hellenic world expressed itself show that the reality is more complex and that not everything is reduced, or reducible, to intellectual categories.

26. Walter Kasper says, with good reason: "Neither the Greek concept [of truth] nor the positivist approach of the exact sciences can serve as the norm for theologians in their effort to express the truth of the gospel" (*Dogme et évangile* [Tournai: Casterman, 1967], p. 57).

27. "The first expression and realization of the Promise was the Covenant" (A. Gelin, *The Key Concepts of the Old Testament* [New York: Sheed and Ward, 1953], p. 37).

28. Reflection on the faith "takes place within the movement of a promise—a promise fulfilled in the course of the historical process, while yet speaking to us of something beyond history" (*Power*, p. 59).

29. *Liberation* p. 92. The entire passage reads as follows: "The Promise is not exhausted by these promises nor by their fulfillment; it goes beyond them, explains them, and gives them their ultimate meaning. But at the same time, the Promise is announced and is partially

and progressively fulfilled in them. There exists a dialectical relationship between the Promise and its partial fulfillments. The resurrection itself is the fulfillment of something promised and likewise the anticipation of a future (cf. Acts 13:23); with it the work of Christ is 'not yet completed, not yet concluded'; the resurrected Christ 'is still future to himself.' The Promise is gradually revealed in all its universality and concrete expression: it is *already* fulfilled in historical events, but *not yet* completely; it incessantly projects itself into the future, creating a permanent historical mobility. The Promise is inexhaustible and dominates history, because it is the self-communication of God. With the Incarnation of the Son and the sending of the Spirit of Promise this self-communication has entered into a decisive stage (Gal. 3:14; Eph. 1:13; Acts 2:38-39; Luke 24:29). But by the same token, the Promise illuminates and fructifies the future of humanity and leads it through incipient realizations towards its fullness."

30. Walter Kasper (n. 26) observes here that "the distinctive thing about the biblical message is that this truth, this value which must be verified, is understood not as an *epiphaneia* or manifestation but as an *epaggelia* or promise" (p. 72).

31. Ibid., pp. 63 and 65. Paul Tillich says something similar: "Truth in Christianity is something that *happens*, something which is bound to a special place, to a special time, to a special personality" (*The Shaking of the Foundations* [New York: Scribner's, 1948], p. 116).

32. *Power*, pp. 12-13: "It is in this framework that the revelation in Jesus Christ is situated—in continuity with the revelation of God in history, but also as an absolute beginning. Jesus Christ is the full manifestation of the God who is love: the Father. He is the fulfillment, and the new departure, of the promise of love. He is the one who bears witness that God is truth. He is the truth of the Father and the key of Scripture."

33. *Power*, p. 19. If the meaning of "God becomes history" is to be correctly understood, the words must not be taken out of their context. In this passage, and in many others, I am emphasizing the irreducibility of God to history. "God becomes history" is synonymous with other expressions which are found in the same book: "God is revealed in history," "God becomes incarnate," "by the incarnation the Son of God becomes part of human history." The immediate context in which I use the phrase shows clearly that there is no danger of immanentism here.

34. Gerhard von Rad, *Old Testament Theology* (New York: Harper, 1965), 2: 338.

35. Gustavo Gutiérrez, *El Dios de la vida* (Lima: U. C., 1982), p. 44. In the same volume, see the commentary on "I am who I am" (Ex.

3:14) and on the theme of God's holiness (pp. 9–13 and 24–26). See also *Liberation*, p. 95.

36. See Vatican II, *Dei Verbum*, no. 2. In connection with the "messianic declaration" in Lk. 4:16–18, John Paul II writes, in his encyclical "Rich in Mercy," that "through such deeds and words Christ makes the Father present in the midst of human beings." On this subject, see H. Echegaray, *The Practice of Jesus* (Maryknoll, N.Y.: Orbis Books, 1984).

37. Tillich (n. 20), p. 116.

38. Karl Lehmann, "Problemas metodológicos y hermenéuticos de la teología de la liberación," in the report of the International Theological Commission, *Teología de la liberación* (Madrid: BAC, 1978), p. 25.

39. Here is another passage, from an earlier encyclical, *Redemptor Hominis*, on concrete respect for human rights: "For this reason the principle of human rights has a profound impact in the area of social justice and becomes a criterion for *judging* whether social justice truly reigns in the life of political institutions" (no. 17, italics added); translated in *The Pope Speaks*, 24 (1979): 128–29.

40. For this reason, the Peruvian bishops write: "The sincerity of our faith must be shown in conduct consistent with it. At the same time, however, we must remember that human beings have an inalienable contemplative dimension that makes them desire knowledge of the truth for its own sake" (*Documento*, no. 43).

41. In voicing their frank acceptance of *LC*, and in commenting on St. John's words "the truth will make them free," Leonardo and Clodovis Boff write: " 'Truth' here is saving truth, the truth that changes us from unjust to just, from people of solitude to people of solidarity, from alienated human beings to friends of God. . . . If we are to know the truth of God as understood by the Bible, we must be converted, do justice, and practice love" ("Convocatoria General em pro da libertação," *Folha de S. Paulo*, May 11, 1986).

42. See, e.g., Jürgen Moltmann's theology of hope or J. B. Metz's political theology.

43. The passages cited are in *Liberation*, pp. 6–8.

44. *Power*, p. 50. The relationship between justice and gratuitousness is a central theme of my book *On Job*.

45. I am therefore far from holding what the Peruvian bishops call "another aspect of Marxist thought," which they describe as "the primacy of praxis: praxis that gives rise to truth or becomes the fundamental criterion of truth" (*Documento*, no. 43).

46. P. Vanzan, "Luci e ombre della teología della liberazione," *La Civiltà Cattolica*, 1985, II: 354–55.

47. In a fine passage, Origen writes: "The soul goes ceaselessly in search of its beloved home; and when it finds it, it again experiences further difficulties and begins to search once more; although it has contemplated this home, it desires that another reveal itself, and when this happens, it desires that the Spouse pass on to things new"; cited in *Los Padres de la Iglesia*, selected and translated by José Vives (Barcelona: Herder, 1971), p. 350.

48. In an interview, Cardinal Ratzinger described the role of the experience of faith as a *locus theologicus* and one of the three factors of doctrinal progress in the church: "There are three main factors of progress in the church: contemplation and study of God's word; the understanding that comes from spiritual experience; and the proclamation of doctrine by the bishops. To this extent the church's tradition gives no evidence of the monopoly, in doctrine and life, that is so often attributed to the episcopal ministry. When we talk of an understanding derived from spiritual experience, we include the whole contribution made by the 'base'—that is, the believing communities, which is recognized as being a *locus theologicus*. On the other hand, it is clear that the three factors are interdependent: experience without reflection is blind; study without experience remains empty; episcopal proclamation that is not rooted in the other two is deprived of effectiveness. The three together build the life of the church; in the course of time one or another of them can take on greater importance, but none of them can be totally absent" (interview on "Luther and the Unity of the Church," in *Documentation catholique*, 81 (1984): 126.

49. I often use this phrase as a synonym for "in the light of faith"; see *Liberation*, passim.

50. *Liberation*, p. 11: "Theology as a critical reflection on Christian praxis in the light of the Word does not replace the other functions of theology, such as wisdom and rational knowledge; rather it presupposes and needs them." Critical reflection on praxis in the light of faith does not, therefore, absorb these other two tasks of theology. In fact, the critical perspective makes rational knowledge a necessity; and the light of faith, which we receive as members of the church, where it is called "the deposit of faith," very much requires a sapiential and spiritual approach.

51. *LN* also acknowledges the fact when it says "the defenders of orthodoxy are sometimes accused of passivity, indulgence, or culpable complicity regarding the intolerable situations of injustice and the political regimes which prolong them." It therefore makes the point regarding these "defenders" that "the concern for the purity of the faith demands giving the answer of effective witness in the service of one's

neighbor, the poor and the oppressed in particular, in an integral theological fashion" (XI, 18).

52. Jon Sobrino points out the connection between these two dimensions in the teaching of Jesus: see his *Christology at the Crossroads. A Latin American Approach* (Maryknoll, N.Y.: Orbis Books, 1978), pp. 57–60. See also my own commentary on this passage of the Bible in my *Drink*.

53. In his nuanced article on liberation theology (n. 46), P. Vanzan writes: "In this sense, liberation theology is a critique of a type of 'ideological' Christianity whose supporters are doctrinally correct, but their faith is not effective in history; in other words, a Christianity that is strong on 'orthodoxy' but deficient in 'orthopraxis' (orthopraxis is Christian activity *in harmony with* the proclamation and requirements of the faith). This type of Christianity, which is dominant in many Christians, including Latin American Christians, contributes to their neglect of temporal and social problems, the privatization of their faith, and the separation of their love of neighbor from commitment to the liberation of the oppressed" (p. 348, note 4). This passage describes the outlook of liberation theology on this subject.

54. Tertullian, *Apologeticum*, XXIV (ed. Onorato Tescari; Turin, 1951, p. 157): "It is criminal impiety to deprive human beings of the freedom of religion and to bar them from their choice of a divinity; that is, not to allow them to worship whomever they wish to worship. No one, not even a human being, wants forced veneration." Lactantius, *Epitome divinarum institutionum*, 54 (PL 6:1061): "Religion is the one place where freedom has chosen to take up residence. Religion depends first and foremost on the will. No one can be forced to worship what he or she does not want to worship."

55. Augustine of Hippo was to give this idea normative status in an incisive formula that has come down the centuries: "No one can believe except willingly" ("*Credere nequis potest nisi volens*") (*Enarrationes in Evangelium Joannis*, 26, 2 [PL 35:1607]).

56. In 457 Pope Leo I wrote to the emperor in Byzantium: "You must realize, and never doubt, that royal power has been given to you not only in temporal affairs but also and above all for the defense of the church" (*Ep.* 21 [PL 54:1130]). The popes of the nineteenth century often cited the words of Leo I.

57. The movement we call liberal Catholicism has been and continues to be extensively studied. Among its outstanding historians are R. Aubert for the French world and A. Jemolo for the Italian. There is a good overview in *Les Catholiques libéraux au XIXe siècle* (Grenoble: Presses Universitaires, 1971); the volume contains the papers of an international conference held in 1971.

58. The scholarly knowledge and great practical sense of Father John Courtney Murray and the man who is now Cardinal Pavan were necessary in order to get around the obstacles created by controverted theological issues and to push the declaration through to acceptance. See G. Gutiérrez, "Tres comentarios a la declaración sobre libertad religiosa," *IDOC* (July 17, 1966).

59. *LC*, no. 8: "The formulation of human rights implies a clearer awareness of the dignity of all human beings. By comparison with previous systems of domination, the advances of freedom and equality in many societies are undeniable."

60. *LC*, no. 19: "Because it has become contaminated by deadly errors about the human condition and human freedom, the deeply rooted modern liberation movement remains ambiguous. It is laden both with promises of true freedom and threats of deadly forms of bondage." A point worth noting here: what this document speaks of as the "modern liberation movement" was often called, in texts of the period and in historical studies of the subject, "the movement for the modern freedoms" that drew its inspiration from the liberalism of the late eighteenth century.

61. See W. Oelmüller, *Die unbefriedigte Aufklärung* (Frankfurt: Suhrkamp Verlag, 1969). The "Frankfurt School" (M. Horkheimer, Th. Adorno, and others) has produced insightful studies of this subject.

62. John Courtney Murray distinguishes between Anglo-Saxon liberalism and continental liberalism (Europe, and France in particular); with regard to the second, he speaks of the danger of a "totalitarian democracy." This approach enables him to attempt an explanation of the unyielding papal opposition to "the modern freedoms" throughout the nineteenth century; see "The Church and Totalitarian Democracy," *Theological Studies* (1952): 525–63.

63. G. de Ruggiero, *Storia del liberalismo europeo* (Milan: Feltrinelli, 1962), p. 43.

64. Hegel has a good description of the situation created by the Enlightenment: "The independent authority of Subjectivity was maintained against belief founded on authority, and the Laws of Nature were recognized as the only bond connecting phenomena with phenomena. Thus all miracles were disallowed: for Nature is a system of known and recognized Laws; Man is at home in it, and that only passes for truth in which he finds himself at home; he is free through the acquaintance he has gained with Nature. Nor was thought less vigorously directed to the Spiritual side of things: Right and [Social] Morality came to be looked upon as having their foundation in the actual present will of Man, whereas formerly it was referred only to the command of God enjoined *ab extra*. . . .

"These general conceptions, derived from actual and present consciousness—the Laws of Nature and the substance of what is right and good, have received the name of *Reason*. The recognition of the validity of these laws was designated by the term *Eclaircissement (Aufklärung)*" (*The Philosophy of History* [New York: Colonial Press, 1900], pp. 440–41).

65. In the final sentence of the cited passage, the Spanish version has "poverty *maintained* by industrial society." The French, which seems to be the original, has *entretenue*, which may be translated as "created *or* caused." The Spanish version does not show a causal relation between industrial society and poverty.

66. René Marlé urges a dialogue between European theology and Latin American theology. For this to occur, the former must (he writes) renounce "a kind of self-sufficiency complex, mixed possibly with some condescension toward these [theological] efforts being made in a region hitherto lacking in any theological tradition of its own. Can theology there possibly be anything other than an application to the local situation of ideas and methods utterly familiar to Europe? ... Recognizable behind this skepticism is not only a Eurocentrism that is very difficult to shake off but also a probably very narrow experience of the 'theological life' and even of theology as such" ("Théologiens en procès," *Recherches de sciences religieuses* [1986]: 95).

67. This error of perspective regarding liberation theology caused me to write, a few years back: "the view that emphasizes the necessity of a liberation of the poor is often interpreted in terms of the debate that has gone on for a long time in Europe (and has intensified in the conciliar and postconciliar periods), between 'conservatives' and 'progressives.' To see how different we here are from the 'progressives' one need only consider how some 'progressives' react to an attitude—and corresponding theology—that focuses on solidarity with the marginalized and exploited of Latin America. Some of these persons find us to be excessively 'traditional' and 'spiritual' and excessively 'church-centered.' The 'conservatives,' of course, pass a different judgment: they see us as reducing everything to the political and as standing to the left of the 'progressivism' they are used to fighting against. In fact, it is increasingly clear to us that these European approaches imprison us in categories that are not ours and that it is impossible for us to carry on a discussion that must pass through the Caudine Forks of the debate between conservatives and progressives. This is a point that calls for further study" ("Por el camino de la Pobreza," *Páginas*, no. 58 [December 1983]; p. 15 of the offprint). See on this point J. Comblin, "A América Latina é o presente debate teológico entre neo-conservadores

e liberais," *Revista Eclesiástica Brasileira*, no. 164 (December 1981): 790–816.

68. In the many theological works being written today in Latin America (most of them adopting the viewpoint of liberation theology) an effort is made to take into account this global situation of the poor. The faith and hope in Jesus that they live out in difficult conditions have a great deal to say to our Christian life and thinking. I am glad therefore to find *LC* saying: "Far from despising or wishing to suppress the forms of popular piety this devotion [to the cross of Jesus] assumes, one should take and deepen all its meaning and implications" (no. 22).

69. Sri Lankan theologian Aloysius Pieris, writing in the context of Asia, speaks of a people both oppressed and religious; see his essay, "Towards an Asian Theology of Liberation: Some Religio-Cultural Guidelines," in Virginia Fabella, ed., *Asia's Struggle for Full Humanity* (Papers from the Asian Theological Conference, January 7–20, 1979, Wennappuwa, Sri Lanka; Maryknoll, N.Y.: Orbis Books, 1980), pp. 75–95.

70. M. Grandona expresses alarm at this "antimodern attitude which is not a dogma of the church"; he claims that "the agreement between the Vatican and the liberation theologians on this point is dangerous because it forms part of the mistrust and disesteem for the scientific, economic, and social progress that is the mark of the present-day world; all this represents a spiritual disposition which it is time to abandon" ("Compromiso en Roma," *Vision*, May 1986).

71. *Power*, p. 203. These lines come toward the end of a section comparing Bultmann and Barth. The former, preoccupied with the difficulty the modern mind has in understanding the message of Christ, "ignores the questions that come from the world of oppression (a world created precisely by the modern person who constitutes his [Bultmann's] point of departure)" (ibid.). On the other hand, "Barth, the theologian of God's transcendence, ... is sensitive to the situation of exploitation in which these broad segments of humanity live" (ibid.). If we had to look among these men for a theologian who has influenced liberation theology, it would undoubtedly be Barth and not Bultmann.

72. See Hugo Echegaray, "Derecho de Dios, derecho de los pobres," in his *Anunciar el Reino* (Lima: CEP, 1981), pp. 54–60.

73. See Gustavo Gutiérrez, "El Reino está cerca," *Páginas*, no. 52 (May 1983).

74. In his Encyclical *Redemptor Hominis* John Paul II has this to say of the key text, Mt. 25:31–46: "This eschatological vision must be constantly related to human history and made the criterion for judging human actions, for it supplies a scheme for self-examination on the

past of each and all" (no. 16; *The Pope Speaks*, 24 [1979]: 125). This idea was later energetically reaffirmed during his trip to Canada in his speech in Edmonton (November 17, 1985).

75. Of the experience, "deeply etched in the soul of society and of the community as well as of individuals," which the Jewish people had of God's mercy, John Paul II writes in his encyclical *Dives in Misericordia*: "Behind the many-faceted conviction of this community and the individuals in it, a conviction shown by the entire Old Testament across the centuries, lies the early experience of the chosen people at the time of the exodus when the Lord saw the wretched state of the enslaved people and, hearing their cry and seeing their affliction, determined to set them free" (no. 4; *The Pope Speaks*, 26 [1981]: 26–27).

76. *LN* rightly points out the danger of reduction to the political: "The liberation of the exodus cannot be reduced to a liberation that is principally or exclusively political in nature" (IV, 3).

77. *Liberation*, p. 89. Along the same line, *LC*, which is aware of the political aspect of the exodus, says: "When God rescues the people from hard economic, political and cultural slavery, God does so in order to make them, through the covenant on Sinai, 'a kingdom of priests and a holy nation' (Ex. 19:6)" (no. 44).

78. In my writings I have often affirmed the primacy of the religious meaning of the exodus. Here are some passages from other works: "The exodus undoubtedly holds an important place in the Bible. It is a foundational event in the history of Israel and as such was constantly reinterpreted. The New Testament too adopts the perspective of the exodus. The theme is therefore an important one. In liberation theology the event of the exodus has a profoundly religious meaning and is a fairly typical example of the relation that exists between political actions and the deeper religious meaning of human history" (*Diálogos en el CELAM* [Bogotá: CELAM, 1974], p. 380).

Liberation deals with the exodus theme in the context of the relation between creation and salvation. It is said there, with all desirable clarity: "Yahweh summons Israel not only to leave Egypt but also and *above all* to 'bring them up out of that country into a fine, broad land; it is a land flowing with milk and honey' (Ex. 3:8). . . . Throughout the whole process, *the religious event* is not set apart. It is placed in the context of the entire narrative, or more precisely, it is its *deepest meaning*. . . . Yahweh liberates the Jewish people politically *in order* to make them a holy nation. . . . The Covenant gives *full meaning* to the liberation from Egypt; one makes no sense without the other. . . . The Covenant and the liberation from Egypt were different aspects of the same movement" (p. 89; italics added).

The same thought is repeated several times elsewhere. "The exodus affords a grasp of the perspective in which the covenant is situated, and the covenant in turn gives full meaning to the liberation from Egypt. *Liberation leads to communion*" (*Power*, pp. 9–10; italics added). "This land in which there will be no exploitation and no need is, in the final analysis, an unmerited gift of the Lord and the pledge of commitment to the people with whom the Lord is establishing a covenant: 'You shall be my people, and I will be your God.' This gift sets everything in motion and leaves its imprint on the process from the beginning" (*Drink*, pp. 78-79).

79. It is perhaps proper for me to note that these other biblical themes (or points) occupy more pages than the exodus does in my works.

80. My debt to this encyclical is explicitly acknowledged in *Liberation*, pp. 162 and 187, note 50. [The translation of *Populorum Progressio* is taken from Joseph Gremillion, *The Gospel of Peace and Justice. Catholic Social Teaching since Pope John* (Maryknoll, N.Y.: Orbis Books, 1976), pp. 387–416.]

81. It was with this in mind that I cited in *Liberation* (104–5) a Latin American text on the missions that concludes with these words: "In him [Christ] and through him salvation is present at the heart of human history, and there is no human act which, in the last instance, is not defined in terms of it" (*La pastoral en las misiones de América Latina* [Bogotá, 1968], 16).

82. Karl Lehmann, "Problemas metodológicos y hermenéuticos de la Teología de la liberación," in *Teología de la liberación* (Madrid: BAC, 1978), pp. 5–6.

83. *Liberation*, p. 103. The passage continues: "Not only is the growth of the kingdom not reduced to temporal progress; because of the Word accepted in faith, we see that the fundamental obstacle to the kingdom, which is sin, is also the root of all misery and injustice; we see that the very meaning of the growth of the kingdom is also the ultimate precondition for a just society and a new humanity. One reaches this root and this ultimate precondition only through the acceptance of the liberating gift of Christ, which surpasses all expectations."

84. *Liberation*, p. 24. The sentences preceding this passage show that only the conquest of sin, which is "a selfish turning in upon oneself," gets at the root.

85. J. C. Scannone makes the same point: "Neither the dualism at work in a distinction of planes (spiritual and temporal) nor any kind of monism (whether sacral or dialectical) fits the structure of the mystery of history which, without confusion or division, is at once profane

and salvific, just as Christ himself (and every other human being in and through him) is, without confusion or division, both son of man and Son of God" (*Teología de la liberación y praxis popular* [Salamanca: Sígueme, 1976], p. 85).

86. The state of the question is clearly given in L. Malevez, "La gratuité du surnaturel," *Nouvelle revue theologique* (1953): 561–68, 673–89, and in G. Colombo, "Il problema del sopranaturale negli ultimi cinquant'anni," in *Problemi ed orientamenti di Teología Dogmatica* (Milan: Carlo Parzorati, 1957), 2:545–608. See also *Liberation*, pp. 43-46.

The work of Cardinal de Lubac played an important part in these discussions. On the erroneous interpretations given of his position during the 1950s, in connection with the publication of the encyclical *Humani Generis* of Pius XII, see his interesting statements in "Viaggio nel Concilio," *30 giorni*, July 7, 1986.

87. See J. Alfaro, *Lo natural y lo sobrenatural. Estudio histórico desde Santo Tomás hasta Cayetano (1274–1534)* (Madrid, 1952); this work is cited in *Liberation*, p. 193, note 22. See the same author's article, "Trascendencia e inmanencia de lo sobrenatural," *Gregorianum*, 38 (1957): 5–50.

88. With skill and sensitivity J. L. Segundo has shown how important it is for our generation to study the second Council of Orange (529), which, following St. Augustine, asserted that the "beginning of faith" is already supernatural; see his *Theology and the Church. A Reply to Cardinal Ratzinger and a Warning to the Whole Church* (London: Chapman, 1985).

89. *Liberation*, p. 44. The expression "affected by grace" alludes to Karl Rahner's well-known thesis concerning the "supernatural existential."

90. As J. C. Scannone (n. 85) says of the theology of liberation: "It rises above a static distinction of planes and instead distinguishes dimensions of one and the same concrete reality, which exists in an eschatological tension ('already' but 'not yet') within a single history" (p. 55).

91. *Liberation*, p. 86: "The Bible establishes a close link between creation and salvation." If there is a link, then there is also difference; otherwise there would be an identity.

92. Ibid. Vatican II emphasized this point in *Gaudium et Spes*, no. 45: "The Lord is the goal of human history, the focal point of the desires of history and civilization, the center of humankind, the joy of all hearts, and the fulfillment of all aspirations. . . . Animated and drawn together in his Spirit we press onward on our journey toward the consummation

of history which fully corresponds to the plan of his love: 'to unite all things in him, things in heaven and things on earth' (Eph. 1:10)" (Flannery, p. 947).

93. After warning against a type of confusionism, Karl Rahner writes in his *Foundations of Christian Faith. An Introduction to the Idea of Christianity* (New York: Seabury, 1978): "The history of the world, then, means the history of salvation. God's offer of himself, in which God communicates himself absolutely to the whole of mankind, is by definition man's salvation. For it is the fulfillment of man's transcendence in which he transcends himself towards the absolute God himself. Therefore the history of God's offer of himself, offered by God in freedom and accepted or rejected by man in freedom, is the history of salvation or its opposite. All other history which can be or has been experienced empirically is really history in the strict sense, and not just the 'history of nature,' only insofar as it is also a genuine moment in this history of salvation or its opposite" (p. 143). Further on, he writes: "The universal history of salvation, which as the categorical mediation of man's supernatural transcendentality is coexistent with the history of the world, is also and at the same time the history of *revelation*. This too, then, is coextensive with the whole history of the world and of salvation" (p. 144).

94. See H. A. Parra, "La teología de la liberación despues de la Instrucción," *Theologica Xaveriana*, no. 73 (October-December 1984): 427: "Since its inception liberation theology has, with G. Gutiérrez, carefully distinguished the three, mutually interrelated levels of meaning of the word 'liberation.'. . . . Several church documents are therefore simply returning to these three levels which liberation theology has from the beginning regarded as obvious." The author alludes, among other texts, to the Puebla documents, 321-329.

95. The theme of the three planes or levels were very much in the mind of Puebla. Here is another passage in which clear reference is made to them: "Thus we mutilate liberation in an unpardonable way if we do not achieve liberation from sin and all its seductions and idolatry, and if we do not help to make concrete the liberation that Christ won on the cross. We do the very same thing if we forget the crux of liberative evangelization, which is to transform human beings into active subjects of their own individual and communitarian development. And we also do the very same thing if we overlook dependence and the forms of bondage that violate basic rights that come from God, the Creator and Father, rather than being bestowed by governments or institutions, however powerful they may be" (no. 485).

96. In Puebla we find similar statements regarding the situation

and its causes. For example: "So we brand the situation of inhuman poverty in which millions of Latin Americans live as the most devastating and humiliating kind of scourge. ... Analyzing this situation more deeply, we discover that this poverty is not a passing phase. Instead it is the product of economic, social, and political situations and structures, though there are also other causes for the state of misery. In many instances this state of poverty within our countries finds its origin and support in mechanisms which, because they are impregnated with materialism rather than any authentic humanism, create a situation on the international level where the rich get richer at the expense of the poor, who get ever poorer" (nos. 29–30).

97. A few lines further on, *LC*, no. 76, says: "Nor can one accept the culpable passivity of the public powers in those democracies where the social situation of a large number of men and women is far from corresponding to the demands of constitutionally guaranteed individual and social rights."

98. *Liberation*, p. 24: "In the first place, [the term] liberation expresses the aspirations of oppressed peoples and social classes, emphasizing the conflictual aspect of the economic, social, and political process, which puts them at odds with wealthy nations and oppressive classes."

99. *LN* I, 6: "The scandal of the shocking inequalities between the rich and the poor—whether between rich and poor countries, or between social classes in a single nation—is no longer tolerated."

100. As does the social teaching of the church, according to *LC*, 72. *LN* had already said quite explicitly: "It is clear that scientific knowledge of the situation and of the possible strategies for the transformation of society is a presupposition for any plan capable of attaining the ends proposed. It is also a proof of the seriousness of the effort" (VII, 3).

101. *Liberation*, p. 30; there is a corresponding passage in *Power*, p. 47. A similar distinction is made in a statement published by the Peruvian episcopal conference: "We think it necessary to state briefly what we mean by 'political.' The political sphere is, *at a first level*, the field in which human beings make themselves masters of their own historical destiny and participate in the orientations of the society to which they belong, in order to make it more just, freer, and more fraternal. The political sphere, thus understood, is a necessary dimension of *every* human action. The presence of the church as a visible historical institution has an *undeniable political dimension* at this first level. At a *second level* there is the choice of a political party; this implies concrete models of social organization, ideologies, and programs for action" (*Documento*

sobre el Sacerdocio ministerial [1971]; italics added).

102. *Liberation*, pp. 66–67. The words "understood in this way" refer to what I gave as the broad meaning; to remove the words would be to invalidate the meaning of the statement.

103. G. Thils, "La portée de l'Instruction sur la théologie de la liberation," *Revue théologique de Louvain*, 15 (1984): 459.

104. *Liberation*, p. 188, note 12 (second part of the note).

105. *Liberation* speaks several times of the "multidimensionality" of human action, precisely in order to avoid an impoverishing unilateral vision of it.

106. "Teología y ciencias sociales," *Páginas*, nos. 63–64 (September 1984): 12.

107. *Liberation*, p. 24. Some pages earlier, I wrote: "To characterize the situation of the poor countries as dominated and oppressed leads one to speak of economic, social, and political liberation. But we are dealing here with a much more integral and profound understanding of human existence and its historical future" (p. 17). Puebla describes as follows what it calls the "second plane": "But the dignity of truly free human beings requires that they not let themselves get locked up in worldly values (Mt. 4:4; Luke 4:4; Deut. 8:3), and particularly in material goods. As spiritual beings, they must free themselves from every sort of servitude to these things. They must move on toward the higher plane of personal relations where they encounter themselves and other human beings" (no. 324).

108. *Liberation*, p. 51. The demand that the person be so understood in every society, of whatever type, is repeated a number of times in unequivocal terms; e.g.: "What is at stake in the South as well as in the North, in the West as well as the East, on the periphery and in the center, is the possibility of enjoying a truly human existence, a free life, a dynamic liberty, which is related to history as a conquest" (ibid., 18).

109. *Power*, p. 47. See *Liberation*, p. 24: "A social transformation, no matter how radical it may be, does not automatically achieve the suppression of all evils"; this passage follows upon the statement that sin is "the ultimate cause of poverty, injustice, and the oppression in which persons live" (ibid.).

110. See "Theology and the Social Sciences": "He [Marx] often presents these economic factors as operating historically in a deterministic manner. I am not concerned here with the important debate on this point, or with the varying interpretations, which this view has occasioned within Marxism itself. The point I want to make is simply that an economically based determinist view of the class struggle is completely alien to liberation theology" (*Páginas*, 11).

111. *Liberation*, p. 21. The places are chosen with a clear intention. Brazil was in that time enduring the worst period of the military dictatorship. The mention of Prague is an allusion to the cruel deeds of the "Prague Spring" of 1968, which was based precisely on this legitimate aspiration for human freedom and fulfillment. That yearning and the terrible repression that it provoked was very much in people's mind during the years when *Liberation* was being written.

112. Archbishop Romero put it well: "The comprehensive plan of liberation which the church proclaims, embraces the entire person in all dimensions, including openness to the absolute that is God. The plan is therefore linked to a particular conception of the human being ... a conception that cannot be sacrificed to the requirements of any strategy, praxis, or short-term success" (Third Pastoral Letter, August 1978).

113. As Paul Ricoeur says: "Only utopia can give economic, social, and political action a human focus" ("Tâches de l'éducateur politique," *Esprit* 33, no. 340 [July-August 1965]: 90; cited in *Liberation*, p. 138).

114. I discuss this matter at length in *Liberation*, pp. 135–40.

115. Both Instructions contain many more passages to the same effect.

116. See the excellent survey of this theme in Francisco Moreno, *Salvar la vida de los pobres* (Lima: CEP, 1986), 117-132.

117. *Liberation*, p. 25. Here is another passage: "Because of the Word accepted in faith, we see that the fundamental obstacle to the kingdom, which is sin, is also the root of all misery and injustice; we see that the very meaning of the growth of the kingdom is also the ultimate precondition for a just society and a new humanity. One reaches this root and this ultimate precondition only through the acceptance of the liberating gift of Christ, which surpasses all expectations" (*Liberation*, p. 103).

Puebla describes the third level of liberation as follows: "However, authentic and permanent attainment of human dignity on this second level would not be possible unless we were at the same time authentically freed to find self-realization on the transcendent level. This is the plane of the Absolute Good, where our freedom is always at stake even when we seem to be unaware of it. It involves an inescapable confrontation with the divine mystery of Someone. As Father, this divine Someone calls human beings, enables them to be free, and guides them providentially. But since they can close themselves to him and even reject him, he also judges them and sentences them to eternal life or eternal death, depending on the freely chosen self-realization of human beings themselves" (no. 325).

118. See the commentary on some of these passages in *Power*, chapter 6.

119. Father Arrupe, one of the great churchmen of our time, explains as follows the failure of Christian spirituality to perceive these social dimensions: "The one thing, I believe, that can be said in explanation of this lacuna in traditional asceticism and spirituality is that human beings have always been more or less aware (with an awareness that Christianity has sharpened) that they can change themselves. . . . On the other hand, *only recently* have they come to understand that the world in which they live, with its structures, organization, ideas, systems, and so on, can also be changed and reformed. . . . The structures of this world, our customs, our social, political, and economic systems, our commercial relations, and, in general, the institutions we ourselves have created, are — to the extent that injustice is interwoven with them — the concrete forms in which sin is objectified" (address at Valencia, July 1973, published in *Vie chrétienne*, no. 178 [June 1975]: 6–7; italics added).

120. Here, as in the discussion of other points, the polemical tone of *LN* gave the impression of greater reserve than was actually felt. But see IV, 14: "Consequently, the full ambit of sin, whose first effect is to introduce disorder into the relationship between God and humankind, cannot be restricted to 'social sin.' The truth is that only a correct doctrine of sin will permit us to insist on the gravity of its social effects." Thus sin indeed has social effects and they are important; *LC* and the encyclical *Reconciliatio et Paenitentia* of John Paul II balance and help us to understand the real scope of the passage just cited.

121. Cardinal Carlo Martini, in his explanation to the synod of the report on "Reconciliation and Penance in the Mission of the Church," said: "As far as the reality of sin is concerned, the report makes clear that it has a social as well as a personal side. Sin always has a social dimension: first, because the will of every human being, and therefore of the sinner, is by its nature directed toward society; second, because sin exerts its influence on social structures, which to some extent bear the mark of human sin (*I.L.*, 12; p. 281). The reference is to objective social situations which are contrary to the gospel and for which persons are always responsible, inasmuch as the situations spring from persons or are due to associations of persons. It is in this sense that we may speak of social sin or 'structural' sin, as some call it. Unjust structures, then, are the fruit of sin; but insofar as they are unjust, they in turn strongly impel human beings to sin"; cited by F. Moreno (n. 117, pp.133–34).

122. John Paul II, apostolic exhortation *Reconciliatio et Paenitentia*,

Section II, Chapter 1, in *The Pope Speaks*, 30 (1985): 41. The whole subsection is devoted to the subject of social sin.

123. A. Bandera, an author with little sympathy for liberation theology, acknowledges the truth of this claim in his *La Iglesia ante el proceso de liberación* (Madrid: BAC, 1975). The emphasis on sin led me to say, in a dialogue on the subject, that "one of the characteristics of a theology of liberation is that it places sin at the center of its thinking, and therefore makes liberation from sin and therefore, too, Christ the redeemer and savior the pivotal point in its approach. The question asked in liberation theology is the connection between this liberation from sin, on the one hand, and political liberation and the liberation of various dimensions of the human, on the other. I am stubborn in my insistence that certain interpretations of liberation theology often forget the distinction between the three levels. The crucial issue is precisely to establish the connection between the several dimensions of a single process of liberation" (*Diálogos en el CELAM*, pp. 379–80). One of the things that sets liberation theology apart from other theologies (many of which adopt a European perspective) is the importance assigned to sin. "In this approach we are far, therefore, from that naive optimism that denies the role of sin in the historical development of humanity. This was the criticism, one will remember, of the Schema of Ariccia and it is frequently made in connection with Teilhard de Chardin and all those theologies enthusiastic about human progress" (*Liberation*, p. 102).

124. *Liberation*, p. 117. Puebla repeats this idea: "liberation *from* all the forms of bondage, from personal and social sin . . . liberation *for* progressive growth in being through communion with God" (no. 482).

125. The new human being of St. Paul is a being who is free with a freedom that, as Romano Guardini put it, "does not at all mean, as extreme eschatologism would have it, that everything on earth and in heaven continues in the power of the old eon and that the new eon can only be hoped for, with a paradoxical faith, in some final state totally different from the present state. No, the new freedom is already here; it was bestowed in baptism and grows through daily Christian life" (*Libertad, gracia y destino* [San Sebastián: Dinor, 1954], p. 73).

126. *LC* speaks, for example, of "the freedom to do good, and in this alone happiness is to be found" (no. 26).

127. *Liberation*, p. 117: "Spirituality, in the strict and profound sense of the word, is the dominion of the Spirit. If 'the truth will set you free' (Jn. 8:32), the Spirit 'will guide you into all the truth' (Jn. 16:13) and will lead us to complete freedom, the freedom from everything that hinders us from fulfilling ourselves as human beings and offspring of

God, and the freedom to love and to enter into communion with God and with others. It will lead us along the path of liberation because 'where the Spirit of the Lord is, there is liberty' (2 Cor. 3:17)."

I have had occasion to expand upon the ideas of *A Theology of Liberation* on this point, in part 3, "Free to Love," of my later book *We Drink from Our Own Wells*. In that book, I say, for example, with regard to the exodus: "The realization of the liberating love of Yahweh had been present from the beginning of the process. At the same time, when this festival of liberation and life was celebrated outside the land of enslavement and death, it served as a means of learning freedom during the crossing of the wilderness and its solitude. The full experience of that freedom was to come in the communion of the promised land" (p. 74).

128. *Liberation*, p. 25. Puebla lends its authority to this view by concluding as follows a lengthy discussion of the subject: "It is from this sin, sin as the destroyer of human dignity, that we must all be liberated. We are liberated by our participation in the new life brought to us by Jesus Christ, and by communion with him in the mystery of his death and resurrection. But this is true only on condition that we live out this mystery on the three planes described above, without focusing exclusively on any one of them. Only in this way will we avoid reducing the mystery to the verticalism of a disembodied spiritual union with God, to the mere existential personalism of individual or small-group ties, or to one or another form of social, economic, or political horizontalism" (no. 329).

129. See Gustavo Gutiérrez, "Haz más de lo que te pido. La Carta a Filemón," *Páginas*, no. 60 (April 1984).

130. As Puebla says: "At the Medellín Conference we saw the elucidation of a dynamic process of integral liberation. Its positive echoes were taken up by *Evangelii Nuntiandi*" (no. 480). Nor should we forget the part played in this development by an important statement of the Peruvian episcopate: *Evangelización: Algunas líneas pastorales* (January 1973).

131. Karl Rahner gives the reasons for this in his book, *The Church after the Council* (New York: Herder and Herder, 1966), p. 138.

132. The Synod of 1985 did the same; see *The Final Report*, II, A.

133. Therefore it must also be at the heart of all theological reflection on the Christian message. The point is one that I have affirmed over and over in my works; see, e.g., *Liberation*, pp. 97ff.; *Power*, p. 69. The point is also present in many other writings which are equally situated in the camp of liberation theology.

134. Yves M.-J. Congar, *Un peuple messianique* (Paris: Cerf, 1975).

135. Congar has always emphasized the value of the expression "people of God" as a description of the church; see, e.g., his essay, "The People of God," in J. Miller, ed., *Vatican II: An Interfaith Appraisal* (Notre Dame, Ind.: University of Notre Dame Press, 1966), 197–207.

136. Congar (n. 135), pp. 95 and 195.

137. Ibid., p. 98.

138. Jürgen Moltmann, *The Church in the Power of the Spirit. A Contribution to Messianic Ecclesiology* (New York: Harper and Row, 1977). The passages cited are on pp. 199-206. According to Dianich, "Estado actual de la eclesiologia," *Concilium*, no. 166 (1981): 461, in this book Moltmann is "very close to liberation theology." See also the stimulating observations of M.-D. Chenu, "Nueva conciencia del fundamento trinitario de la Iglesia," ibid., pp. 340–63.

139. John Paul II has repeatedly recalled this role of the church as defender of human dignity. On the presence of this theme in his Latin American addresses, see C. I. González, "La teología de la liberación a la luz del magisterio de Juan Paul II en América Latina," *Gregorianum*, 67 (1986).

140. In this paragraph, and in some others further on, I have used my article, "Por el camino de la pobreza," *Páginas*, no. 58 (December 1983).

141. The complete text reads: "The church in Latin America should be manifested, in an increasingly clear manner, as truly *poor, missionary*, and *paschal*, separate from all temporal power and courageously committed to the liberation of each and every person" (*Youth*, 15a; italics added).

142. See John Paul II, Address to the Peruvian Bishops (October 4, 1984).

143. In these pages on the evangelizing potential of the poor, I make use of my essay, "The Church and the Poor: A Latin American Perspective," in G. Alberigo, J.-P. Jossua, and J. A. Komonchak, eds., *The Reception of Vatican II* (Washington, D.C.: Catholic University of America Press, 1987), pp. 171–93.

144. See Gustavo Gutiérrez, "El Evangelio del trabajo," in *Sobre el trabajo humano* (Lima: CEP, 1982), pp. 11–63. According to the Peruvian bishops, this encyclical opened up "a whole route which our church must travel in evangelizing the world of work amid the entire social structure encasing it" (*Documento*, no. 30).

145. *Power*, p. 50 (passage already cited in the first part of this essay).

146. This was the perspective adopted by Y. Calvez in his important work, *Eglise et société économique* (2 vols.; Paris: Aubier, 1959 and 1963).

147. Ricardo Antoncich's study in his *Christians in the Face of Injustice. A Latin American Reading of Catholic Social Teaching* (Maryknoll, N.Y.: Orbis Books, 1987), pp. 84-126, is the best thing available on this subject from the viewpoint of the problems facing the Latin American church and the theology being done among us.

148. Calvez, *Eglise*, 1:262. R. Antoncich tells us that "the confusion between the natural right of use and the positive right of ownership, thus making the latter a natural right, was due to Luigi Taparelli (1793–1862)" (*Christians*, p. 125).

149. Calvez, *Eglise* 1:271-78.

150. *LC* had hardly been published when some of the media were claiming that the Instruction had replaced "preferential option" with "preferential love" and that this supposed shift signified a break with what had been said earlier by Medellín, Puebla, and John Paul II. There is certainly no basis for the claim. Furthermore, the pope has continued to use that expression in texts subsequent to the Instruction.

151. Here are two passages: "This is what the theology of liberation had attempted to do, both before Medellín and after. For the reasons noted, no exclusivity is ever affirmed. Instead, Puebla emphasizes a preference, stressing the special place the poor have in the message of the Bible and in the life and teaching of Jesus and the position they therefore ought to occupy among those who consider themselves his disciples. From this point of departure it is possible to proclaim the gospel to *every* human being" (*Power*, p. 129). "Universal love and preference for the poor distinguish the message of the divine reign that both purifies human history and transcends it" (*On Job*, p. 97).

152. The Bible is always read and reread in the Christian community in light of the challenges its evangelizing work must meet at the particular historical moment. John Paul II said, in this regard: "The church has since its beginnings continually meditated on these texts and messages, but it is conscious that it has still not plumbed them as it wants to (will it perhaps some day reach this goal?). In differing concrete situations it *rereads* these texts and scrutinizes this message because it desires to make a new application of them" (Homily at Salvador, Bahía, July 7, 1980, in *Pronunciamentos do Papa no Brasil* [São Paulo: Loyola, 1980]: 192; italics added). This is the meaning of the term "rereading" that is often used in biblical studies, whence it was taken over by liberation theology.

153. On this subject see J. Dupont, *Les Béatitudes* (Paris: Gabalda, 1969).

154. The poor are the uninvited of history and therefore are called first to the kingdom; see J. Dupont, "La parabola del ministerio de

Jésus," in *La parabola degli invitati al banchetto* (Brescia, 1978).

155. I owe these observations to J. Linskens, professor of Sacred Scripture at the Mexican American Cultural Center in San Antonio, Texas.

156. On this see *Power*, pp. 137–39, and *El Dios de la Vida*, pp. 87–88.

157. For what follows I am using, with some alterations, my article "Ser discípulo segun Mateo," *Páginas*, no. 76 (April 1986).

158. *LC*, no. 62: "The Beatitudes, beginning with the first, the one concerning the poor, form a whole which itself must not be separated from the entirety of the Sermon on the Mount. In this sermon Jesus, who is the new Moses, gives a commentary on the Decalogue, the law of the covenant, thus giving it its definitive and fullest meaning."

159. An interesting fact: In the Greek text each half has thirty-six words; this gives an idea of the care which the author bestowed on the redaction of the text.

160. *LC* says: "The Beatitude of poverty that he proclaimed can never signify that Christians are permitted to ignore the poor, who lack what is necessary for human life in this world. This poverty is the result and consequence of human sin and natural frailty, and it is an evil from which human beings must be freed as completely as possible" (no. 67). The negative phrasing and the somewhat defensive tone do not make it sufficiently clear that, far from urging disinterest toward the poor, the Beatitude on poverty necessarily implies a solidarity with them. See the beautiful commentary John Paul II gave on the Beatitudes in Vidigal, a poor neighborhood of Rio de Janeiro (July 2, 1980).

161. As is generally known, this idea was a contribution of the Peruvian episcopate at Puebla.

162. Radio Message of September 11, 1962, in F. Anderson, ed., *Council Daybook, Vatican II, Sessions 1 and 2* (Washington, D.C., 1965), pp. 18–21. John XXIII liked the image of the "luminous point" for emphasizing the importance of an idea; see his announcement of the council (January 25, 1959) and his *Journal of a Soul*.

163. See the complete text of this statement in G. Lercaro, *Per la forza dello Spirito. Discorsi conciliari* (Bologna: Edizio di Dehoniane, 1984), pp. 109-122.

164. A little later on, Cardinal Lercaro took the same clear and profound theological approach to poverty in his preface to *Eglise et pauvreté* (Paris: Cerf, 1965).

165. On this point, Puebla (no. 1146) cites the council's decree *Apostolicam Actuositatem*, no. 8: "Not only the effects but also the causes of various ills must be removed."

166. On the three meanings of the word "poor," see *Liberation*, chapter 13 (pp. 162–73).

167. The pope has returned several times to the theme of the "church of the poor"; see A. Barreiro, *Os pobres e o Reino. Do Evangelho a João Paulo II* (São Paulo: Loyola, 1983).

168. This statement is repeated several times in the same document (see no. 18) and in other "conclusions" of Medellín.

169. In the beginning, the term "popular church" or "church of the people" was used for "church of the poor," which expresses the vocation of the entire church and is not intended as an alternative to it. For this reason, one also spoke of "the church that is born of the people under the action of the Spirit" (see Puebla, no. 263). Today, in light of the misuses and the mistaken interpretations, the expression "people's church" must definitely be discarded (Puebla already said that it is "quite unfortunate" because of its ambiguity and the strange interpretations given of it). Its use today can only produce needless confusion.

170. Karl Barth, *Kirchliche Dogmatik*, II, 1, p. 434.

171. Sole document produced by the Thirty-third General Congregation of the Society of Jesus (1983), no. 36.

172. *Liberation*, xiii. These are the opening words of the Introduction to the first edition.

173. In an article, "Aun es tiempo," *La República*, June 25, 1986, I have tried to reflect on this distressing situation and on rejection of the violence current in Peru.

Index